POEMS

&

COUNSELS ON PRAYER
AND CONTEMPLATION

for Clara, Selevan, and Abram

Poems
&
Counsels on Prayer
and Contemplation

DAME GERTRUDE MORE

edited and introduced by

Jacob Riyeff

GRACEWING

First published in England in 2020
by
Gracewing
2 Southern Avenue
Leominster
Herefordshire HR6 0QF
United Kingdom
www.gracewing.co.uk

The publishers have no responsibility for the persistence or
accuracy of URLs for websites referred to in this publication,
and do not guarantee that any content on such websites is, or
will remain, accurate or appropriate.

ISBN 978 085244 943 1

Typeset by Word and Page, Chester, UK
Cover design by Bernardita Peña Hurtado

CONTENTS

Sir Thomas More[1]

magnes amoris amor[2]

Renownèd More, whose bloody fate
England ne'er yet could expiate,
such was thy constant faith, so much
thy hope, thy charity was such,
as made thee twice a martyr prove:
of faith in death, in life of love!
View here thy grandchild's broken heart,
wounded with a seraphic dart.
Who, while she lived mortals among,
thus to her Spouse Divine she sung:
'Mirror of Beauty, in whose Face
the essence lives of ev'ry grace!
True lustre dwells in thy sole sphere;
those glimm'rings that sometimes appear
in this dark vale, this gloomy night,
are shadows tipped with glow-worm light.
Shew me thy radiant parts above,
where angels unconsumèd move,
where am'rous fire maintains their lives
as man by breathing air survives.
But if perchance the mortal eye
that views thy dazzling looks must die,
with blind faith here I'll kiss them and desire
to feel the heat before I see the fire'.

---

[1]   This poem addressed to Saint Thomas More (Dame Gertrude More's great-great-grandfather) serves as the dedicatory poem appended to the version of Dame Gertrude's works printed in 1658—who composed it is uncertain.

[2]   'Love attracts love': *magnes* is literally a lodestone (a magnetic stone), but its attractive force is what is central to the proverbial saying here. In the 1658 printed version, this motto appears below Dame Gertrude's portrait across the page from this dedicatory poem.

FOREWORD

What sort of person does the word 'poet' suggest? Perhaps a 'head in the clouds' type, or someone of a rather dreamy disposition. Dame Gertrude More (1606–33) does not fit this stereotype. One of the founding nuns of the seventeenth-century English Benedictines in Cambrai, Flanders (who now live in Yorkshire, England), she was, for most of her short life, the community's cellarer, that is, she had responsibility for the material and financial side of the monastery. Yet, after what was evidently a very holy death from smallpox at the age of twenty-seven, Dame Gertrude left behind some deeply spiritual writings, including the poems and 'Apology' collected here.

We should not be surprised at this only apparent paradox, for the Benedictine Rule under which Dame Gertrude lived promotes such an integration of the material and the spiritual, the rational and the affective, which is, after all, the pattern of the Incarnation: 'The Word became flesh', God becoming fully human. Such integration is, therefore, the pattern for all Christian lives.

Jacques Maritain's definition of poetry as 'the divination of the spiritual in the things of sense and which expresses itself in the things of sense' ('The Frontiers of Poetry', *Art and Scholasticism*) finds a more down-to-earth echo in the Rule of Saint Benedict, which states that 'all the tools and utensils of the monastery are to be regarded as sacred vessels of the altar' (RB 31.10).

This was the ethos under which Dame Gertrude had been trained and lived out her monastic life. Then, like any Benedictine monk or nun, she was steeped in the Scriptures, heard in the liturgy and pondered every day in *lectio divina*. Benedictines are especially immersed in the Psalms, those poems of the People of Israel which form the backbone of the daily choral monastic Offices. Further, both in the Office and personal reading, the nuns had access to the writings of the Fathers of the Church, rich in allegory and alert to the multiple levels of meaning in a text, including the text of the sixth-century Rule which Benedictines follow to this day. So, in a poem addressed to Saint Benedict (printed in full on pp. 21–3 below), Dame Gertrude could write:

vii

> The more I look upon thy Rule,
> the more in it I find.
> O do to me the sense unfold
> for letter makes us blind!

While Dame Gertrude was undoubtedly blessed with a gift for poetry—even as a girl she used to answer her father in rhymes—the Benedictine life that she lived, and which is lived today across the globe, lends itself to the poetic. Indeed, insofar as the Benedictine life incarnates and makes visible the life of Jesus Christ, that life itself is poetic.

It is probably more unusual for a nun to write an 'Apology'. But, for the privileged insights into both the prayer of Dame Gertrude and the spiritual guidance of her mentor, Dom Augustine Baker (1575–1641) which this text affords, we can be grateful that she did and that it has come down to us. For while the seventeenth-century controversy which occasioned the 'Apology' (see pp. 29–37 below) is likely to be of interest mainly to specialists, very many will surely welcome this first-hand account of the inner life of contemplative prayer to which all Christians are called to some degree. Then, of course, the spirit of attention to the voice of conscience which it manifests, so marked in Saint Thomas More, ancestor of Dame Gertrude, speaks to people in every season.

Some words from 'The Elixir' of the great English priest-poet George Herbert (b. 1593), who died just a few months before Dame Gertrude in 1633, might serve as a fitting preface to her own poems as well as epitomizing her approach to prayer:

> Teach me, my God and King,
> In all things thee to see,
> And what I do in any thing
> To do it as for Thee ...
>
> A man that looks on glasse,
> On it may stay his eye;
> Or, if he pleaseth, through it passe,
> And then the heav'n espie ...

We owe a debt of gratitude to Jacob Riyeff and to Gracewing for making these precious writings of Dame Gertrude More accessible to a wider audience. May her spiritual legacy help us re-connect with the contemplative impulse in our own lives so that 'in all things God may be glorified' (RB 57.9).

Laurentia Johns, OSB
Stanbrook Abbey, Yorkshire

Epiphanytide, 2020

ACKNOWLEDGEMENTS

This project began with a summer seminar on Medieval Women Mystics and Visionaries I taught at Marquette University—first thanks go to my students in that class who taught me how to teach mysticism and who first read Dame Gertrude's works with me.

My gratitude also goes to the community at Stanbrook Abbey who helped shepherd this collection into publication, especially Abbess Anna Brennan, Dame Laurentia Johns, and Dame Philippa Edwards. Special thanks to Sister Gertrude Feick of the Abbey of Our Lady of the Redwoods, who saw potential in the project and put me in contact with Gracewing. Dr Emily Ransom, as usual, came through with much-needed assistance—this time acquiring images of the Rawlinson manuscript of Dame Gertrude's poems and reading through the introduction to catch any infelicities as I (a medievalist) talked about the early modern period. Tom Longford at Gracewing had confidence in this project from the get-go and has been a pleasure to work with. Fr Aaron Pidel, SJ, came through quickly with help on Jesuit constitutions—my sincere appreciation for not having to source that one on my own! It is my great pleasure also to thank my daughter, Clara, for our first collaboration—her help editing 'The Simple Exercise of the Will' was both beyond her paygrade as a seven-year-old as well as a total delight!

Finally, my deepest appreciation as ever goes to Sr Pascaline Coff, OSB, for inviting me into the Benedictine world so welcomingly and to my wife, Mamie, for her continual support and selfless love.

Jacob Riyeff, OblSB
Marquette University
Milwaukee, Wisconsin, USA

Feast of Saint Meinrad, 2020

INTRODUCTION

Let us not seek the gift but the Giver.
Let us seek no other comfort but to be able,
without all comfort, to be true to him.

Dame Gertrude More, 'Apology'

Dame Gertrude (*née* Helen) More, born at Low Leyton, Essex, in 1606, lived her entire adult life in voluntary exile. From 1623 she dwelt hidden from the world in the cloister of the Benedictine Abbey of Our Lady of Comfort in Cambrai, which she co-founded. In 1633, she died prematurely and peacefully of smallpox at twenty-seven years of age. She never published anything during her lifetime. As far as we know, she never left the cloister after she entered its walls. Such, perhaps, does not seem a likely life to impress us. Yet, as with so many disciples of Christ, who 'emptied himself [and] humbled himself, becoming obedient to death' (Phil 2:7–8), she possessed 'the same attitude' and emptied herself. In giving up 'houses or brothers or sisters or father or mother or children or lands for the sake' of Christ's name, she received 'a hundred times more' (Matt 19:29). That is perhaps all that needs to be said about her to recommend her to our attention.

But there is more. Amidst her short twenty-seven years, she was a key figure in the refounding of female English Benedictine monasticism after the ruptures and violence of the sixteenth-century reformations. She was a close and primary disciple of Dom Augustine Baker, one of the recognized masters of the contemplative life as the world drifted toward modernity. She wrote with profundity concerning her own spiritual tradition and with psychological acuity concerning her interior life in a day when few women were writers, let alone were published. By all counts she appears to have enjoyed profound contemplative union with God, having dedicated her life to prayer, silence, and mortification, like so many monastics before and after her. And she was a living link in the chain of monastic spirituality and Christian contemplation at a crucial moment in history, when the organic monastic tradition of the ancient and medieval worlds was acutely threatened from different quarters.

The poems and prose texts presented here give us a privileged view into the inner world of Dame Gertrude More. The tone and the material she treats in this work might lead a reader to think she had a very quiet and reserved personality. (Though the outspokenness of her 'Apology' is one signal otherwise.) On the contrary, her contemporaries report that she was generally a cheerful and extroverted person, overall a source of great inspiration and encouragement to the nuns at Cambrai. As a child she was energetic and at times answered her father in rhymes, an early sign of her skill with rhyme demonstrated in the poems below. In the monastery, we are also told, she was eager for the business of the house, spoke with visitors often at the grate, enjoyed conversation with her sisters, and wrote many letters—she was clearly of a strong and independent spirit. After 1629, she was a close helper to the newly elected abbess, became the community's cellarer in charge of the material goods of the monastery, and was responsible for the lay sisters of the community. Given all this, when reading Dame Gertrude's works we should not mistake seriousness for dourness or mistake a contemplative disposition for one that was aloof. As a good daughter of Saint Benedict, our sources suggest that as she 'progressed in the monastic life' her 'heart overflowed with the inexpressible delight of love' (Rule of Saint Benedict [RB] Prol.49).

Dame Gertrude is then one point of light in a constellation of female monastics and mystics like Saint Hildegard, Saint Mechthild, Saint Gertrude the Great (her namesake in religion), Saint Catherine of Sienna, and so many others—each their own star but forming a larger picture together. This larger picture is a witness to the life of the Blessed Trinity supporting all of existence and poured into our hearts, sustained over centuries and overcoming all manner of adversity and limitation.

It is important to note as well that this larger picture is one made primarily of concepts and images straining not to form intellectual points, but rather to express and articulate lived experience. The great Benedictine scholar, Jean Leclercq, while cautioning against too hard a distinction, made much of the difference between monastic theology and scholastic theology. In Leclercq's reckoning of monastic theology, 'in study and in reflection importance was granted to the inner illumination of which Origen and St. Gregory spoke so often, to that grace of intimate prayer, ... that manner of savoring and relishing the Divine realities which is constantly taught in the patristic tradition.'[1] This form of theology allowed for the use of reason but always maintained that, to genuinely gain a coherent and unified view of the faith, 'there is no need to resort to any ideas gleaned from extraneous sources' beyond the Bible and the teaching of the Fathers.[2]

Monastic theology, which endured virtually unrivalled in the west for hundreds of years, emphasized the practical reality of the moral reformation of life and the training of the attention in prayer that led, ultimately, to contemplative union with God—and the intimate relationship of the two. Dame Gertrude was, for the seventeenth century anyhow, a well-educated woman. Whether or not she would have been capable of academically sophisticated theology is of course unknowable, but it should be made clear that it is not only because of her station as a young enclosed nun that she wrote the way she did. The experiential and practical focus of monastic theology had a long tradition before her, a stream into which she seems to have entered confidently—at least once the rockiness of her early years at the monastery had abated. Her wisdom (knowledge known through participation and experience) speaks to us as a sure guide along paths already trodden, paths toward contemplative union with the Blessed Trinity.

In taking on the centuries-old practices of monastic life and contemplative prayer—newly expressed for her age but perennially the same at root—Dame Gertrude lived as part of a movement that bequeathed that ancient tradition to a world changed by the sixteenth-century reformations and the Scientific Revolution. This world was also well on its way to the Enlightenment and Industrial Revolution, inching toward modern nation states and rampant consumerism. In her humble and simple—yet forceful and earnest— poems and counsels on prayer and contemplation, she not only entered the stream of monastic culture that has persisted in the west since the fourth century. She also took on the active role of passing

---

[1]   Jean Leclercq, *The Love of Learning and the Desire for God: A Study of Monastic Culture* (New York: Fordham University Press, 1982), p. 213.
[2]   Ibid., p. 215.

that tradition on to others through the lens of her own interactions with and embodiment of it. It is with great joy and hope that I pass these works along to a wider audience in this book.

BENEDICTINE MONASTICISM IN ENGLAND[3]

The contribution of Dame Gertrude and her early-seventeenth century sisters will be much clearer if we have a greater understanding of the long development and importance of monasticism in the western Church and the great rupture that came with the sixteenth-century reformations, especially as these developed in England. Reaching back to the early Anglo-Saxon period, when Germanic tribes occupied much of the island of Britain and pushed the earlier Celtic inhabitants more or less to its outer territories, Pope Saint Gregory the Great (†604) sent a mission to convert the Anglo-Saxons to Christianity. This mission was headed by Saint Augustine of Canterbury (†604), a Roman monk of Saint Gregory's own monastery. When the mission arrived in Britain, the Church that began to grow in England had a particularly monastic character, passing on the inheritance of the Desert Fathers and Mothers, Saint John Cassian, Saint Benedict, Saint Columban, and Saint Martin of Tours to these largely illiterate peoples who lived on 'the edge of the world'. Though the Rule of Saint Benedict was known early on in England, monasticism was still a looser institution then than it would later become, and the monasteries of England were not yet 'Benedictine' in the modern sense. Monastic life developed in more and less rigourous forms. Strict enclosure and a complete separation from secular affairs remained relatively uncommon in England's early 'minsters'.

However, in the wake of serious changes in monasticism on the continent, English monasticism began changing into what we would

---

[3]   Historical information and basic interpretation in this and the following sections is taken from the following publications: *Stanbrook Abbey: A Sketch of Its History 1625–1925*; Dom David Knowles, *The Religious Orders in England*, pp. 421–55; The Benedictines of Stanbrook, *In a Great Tradition*; Frideswide Sandeman, *Dame Gertrude More*; Claire Walker, *Gender and Politics in Early Modern Europe*; and Martin Heale, *Monasticism in Late Medieval England, c. 1300–1535*, pp. 1–74.

call a distinctly 'Benedictine' form in the tenth century. When the Emperor Charlemagne (†814) began to shore up his new empire on the Continent, he recognized how helpful the monasteries could be as islands of learning and order throughout his lands. Though he set policies in motion to take advantage of the monasteries, general standardization of the monastic life (following the Rule of Saint Benedict and centered especially on the elaborate celebration of the liturgy) would wait for Charlemagne's son, Louis the Pious (†840), and Saint Benedict of Aniane's (†821) reforms in the early ninth century. These reforms of monasticism were renewed and spread throughout the ninth and early tenth century, until, eventually, they spread to England.

After King Alfred (†899) had turned the tide against the Vikings (who had upset English society so much throughout the ninth century), his heirs began to centralize England's institutions. King Edgar the Pacific (†975), along with the monastic reformers Saints Dunstan (†988), Æthelwold (†984) and Oswald (†992), reformed monasticism in England: refounding old monasteries, founding new ones, and recruiting many new monastics to fill these communities. While the monasteries had always enjoyed the patronage of the king and other nobility, the association of monastics and the Crown now became much stronger and more direct as the reform sought to carve out a space for monastic life relatively free of the control of local secular lords. King Edgar and the three monastic bishops brought monks from the Benedictine houses on the Continent to help guide the Benedictine character of this new wave of monastic life in the kingdom, with great success. Monasteries became centers of learning, liturgy, and the arts and hubs of social and political power throughout England.

In the high and later Middle Ages, this firm basis was further reformed and shored up, with some Benedictine houses enduring for centuries and becoming some of the largest landowners in the kingdom (though it should be remembered that many smaller houses—especially women's houses—struggled greatly). In the wake of the Conquest in 1066, monasteries generally fared well; though, like the secular lords, their superiors were replaced by and large by Anglo-Normans. As centuries advanced, monasteries became more and more embedded within the social fabric of the kingdom—its economy, its governing structure, and its religious and spiritual habits. As it did so, monastic life on the ground developed and changed. Most notably, the Fourth Lateran Council (1215) decreed that the Benedictines would adopt a system of general chapters for governance similar to those of the Cistercians; the Council of Vienne (1311–12) set forth new standards for dress, diet, authority structures, and other customs; and Pope Benedict XII's bull *Summi magistri* (1336), supported by English chapter recommendations, permitted meat-eating within limits, reduced liturgical observance, and encouraged study at university. Whatever one thinks of these changes, they re-shaped the nature and rhythm of medieval monastic life in substantial ways.

On the eve of the Henrician Reformation, it has popularly been accepted that monasticism was on its last leg, a corrupt and bloated social institution with little practical benefit; this understanding of history has thankfully been challenged in the last few decades. In part, scholars have been more ready to acknowledge that the accusations and rhetoric used to justify the Dissolution of the Monasteries (1536–41) under King Henry VIII (†1547) were just that—'spin' to justify the breaking up of age-old institutions and the claiming of their assets for the Crown. To be fair, it is clear that the populace of England did at times have genuine qualms with the monasteries (as disenfranchised populations tend to have with large landholders), evidenced by various revolts and complaints throughout the middle ages. Yet while these skirmishes did occur and there is evidence of a lack of rigour and of corruption in some monasteries, we also find evidence for monasticism's value and continued relevance. In particular, monastic profession continued unabated until the Dissolution, construction continued in some monasteries up until the Dissolution, and laity continued to seek out confraternity with the monasteries as well. Enrolment in confraternity (whereby laity share in the good works and prayers of a particular monastery and which is an 'ancestor' of the modern lay Benedictine oblates) evinces in particular the continued desire for the exchange of prayers and support among laity and monastic communities that reaches back into the distant past and continues to the present day, resisting the tides of history and fashion. The importance of the monastic life for the Church was and is signalled clearly in the solidarity that monastics and non-monastic Christians find with one another, each group supporting one another with a delicate balance of work and prayer in the vineyard (Matt 20:1–16).

With the Dissolution of the Monasteries and the Act of Supremacy under Henry VIII, the monasteries disbanded. Their property was alienated and their inmates were either martyred (for refusing the Oath of Supremacy) or capitulated to the new wave of power (often with reliably comfortable means of support from the Crown). Under Henry's daughter Mary I (†1558), religious life would find a brief regeneration in England, but it would not last. With the accession of Mary in 1553 and her partnership with the papal legate Reginald Cardinal Pole (†1558), several religious houses were set up. The legal situation of the property alienated from the monasteries during Henry's reign was sticky. But, after a parliamentary petition, Pole's endorsement, and the papal bull *Praeclara* (1555), the old rights to the land were formally dissolved so that a new branch could grow from the old stock.

With regards to the Benedictines, Mary installed sixteen former monks of various houses to a newly founded Westminster Abbey in 1556. Though the present introduction will not enter into the legal intricacies of this move, the spirit of the English Benedictines, if not a corporate legal entity, was here renewed.[4] However, after a brief life Westminster was once again dissolved, this time by Elizabeth I (†1603) in 1559. Though the results seem almost inevitable in hindsight, where the winds would ultimately blow the Church in England was still very much a live question at the time.

As it turned out, the new wave of English Benedictine life that would endure uninterruptedly to the present began outside the borders of England, on the continent, with self-imposed exiles (like Dame Gertrude More and her sisters at Cambrai). For the space of around thirty years, those English who sought out ministerial roles in the Church were men who went to study for the secular priesthood at English colleges on the Continent (like Douai, founded in 1568) or for the religious priesthood in the new Society of Jesus (the Jesuits). But as tensions and infighting grew in the ranks of

---

[4] Br Ambrose Bennett explores these perspectives on the origins of the modern English Benedictine Congregation in his essay, '"Modernist" History versus Monastic History: The Continuity of the English Benedictines', *The Downside Review* 118.412 (2000), pp. 199–220.

these groups, some Englishmen saw the older monastic order as a way both to contribute to the Catholic cause and to lead a religious life deep in tradition—relatively free of the problems besetting the colleges. These new recruits to the monastic life went to the monasteries of Italy (especially the Cassinese Congregation) and Spain (especially the Congregation of Valladolid), houses that were fervent in the new Catholic Reformation spirit and had been reformed in the late-medieval period. Permission for these Benedictines to undertake the mission to England was granted by Pope Clement VIII in 1602. In 1603, English Benedictines returned to England in two waves, reviving monasticism in the country for the first time since the dissolution of Westminster in 1559.

The gathering of the monks belonging to foreign congregations into an English Benedictine Congregation was a difficult and unprecedented task. The legal and hierarchical questions were genuine ones, and it seems that no one knew exactly how to proceed—even the question of whether the Congregation would be 'continued', 'renewed', or 'erected' was unsure. Different monks pursued different avenues. One major plan (known as 'the Buckley affair') was to 'continue' the Congregation via a legal association with the last remaining Westminster monk, Fr Sigebert Buckley. However, in the end the different approaches were irrelevant, as Pope Paul V's brief *Ex incumbenti* (1619) established the English Benedictine Congregation under whatever legal guise the situation actually demanded (though it never claims what that situation is!). And so, the four original priories of the modern English Benedictine Congregation—Saint Gregory's at Douai (1606), which would later become Downside Abbey; Saint Laurence's at Dieulouard (1608), which would later become Ampleforth Abbey; Saint Benedict's at Saint Malo (1611), which would later be handed over to the French Congregation of Saint-Maur; and Saint Edmund's at Paris (1615) which later became Douai (Woolhampton)—were brought together into one body, and the Benedictine life among the English found new and continuing life. From its earliest, inchoate origins to its deep complicity in the feudal structures of medieval England to its precarious renewal in exile—and with due acknowledgement that plenty of monks likely fell short of their order's ideal—monasticism's witness to total sacrifice for the Kingdom of God, to silence, to the primacy of the liturgy, and to the value of the contemplative life all survived, and do survive to the present day. Continuity amidst disruption characterizes the institution of monasticism in England, as everywhere, preserving essentials even as particulars are forced to adapt to a variety of social pressures.

THE ABBEY OF OUR LADY OF COMFORT

In the wake of the Henrician Reformation, those English desiring to remain in communion with Rome were beset with obstacles and the need to find new patterns of individual and common life. As seen above, in the wake of the Dissolution of the Monasteries, there was no opportunity for the monastic life to continue within England. After Mary's brief resuscitation of Benedictine life between 1556–9, the situation was even more stark, though people continued to hold onto the hope that Roman communion might once more return to England. Even before the English Benedictine priories for men were founded in France and Flanders, Lady Mary Percy (†1642) co-founded with two other English women the Benedictine Abbey of the Glorious Assumption of Our Blessed Lady in Brussels in 1598. This new Benedictine community enjoyed a good reputation, but it was also stricken with discord early on due to conflicts surrounding spiritual direction—conflicts which would also beset the Cambrai community and Dame Gertrude in particular, as we will see below. All told, seven Benedictine convents were founded in exile (along with fifteen others of various orders), some moving back to England during troubles on the continent, others closing. But only the Abbey of Our Lady of Comfort at Cambrai was initially founded under the direct authority of the English Benedictine Congregation, the others being placed under the authority of local bishops.

The Abbey of Our Lady of Comfort was founded by nine young Englishwomen, led by Dame Gertrude More, who were clothed in the Benedictine habit on December 31, 1623. The new community was at first guided by three Benedictines from the Brussels convent. Through these women and their formation at Brussels, Jesuit forms of meditation and prayer (imaginative and sensual discursive meditations based in late-medieval piety) were brought into the community. Such forms of piety in part reflected anxiety during the Catholic Reformation regarding less rigorously guided forms of devotion. These practices created problems for the novices that echoed similar dissatisfaction with Jesuit methods among members of the Brussels community. Accordingly, the Cambrai nuns sent an appeal to the President of the English Benedictine Congregation, Dom Rudesind Barlow (†1656), to provide a monk who could train the novices in the Benedictine life of contemplation. Dom Augustine Baker (†1641) was sent to teach and form the novices in the contemplative life in 1624. His guidance on the path of prayer and contemplation eventually galvanized the community and brought, especially, the spiritual lives of Dames Gertrude More and Catherine Gascoigne (one of the original founders and long-time abbess of the community) to fruition.

Dom Augustine Baker stayed until 1633, when his teachings came under suspicion through conflict with the convent's vicar, Dom Francis Hull (†1645, appointed vicar in 1629). Dom Francis saw the attention the nuns gave to Dom Augustine's teaching—and that teaching itself—as contrary to his authority. As tensions rose, the two monks were ordered to the General Chapter of 1633 and Dom Augustine's doctrine was assessed. Dames Gertrude and Catherine were also asked to submit testimonies of their prayer lives and Dom Augustine's guidance. Dom Augustine was vindicated but assigned to Saint Gregory's at Douai and would never return to Cambrai. Dame Gertrude contracted smallpox and died during the Chapter and would not see Dom Augustine again. Dame Gertrude's death must have cast a pall over the community, but, with Dom Augustine's and the nuns' vindication, a spiritual 'school' began to take shape at Cambrai. With this approbation of their spiritual lives and with an abbess chosen from their own ranks (Dame Catherine was elected in 1629), the community emerged with a strong foundation for the troubled years ahead.

While the monastery endured and the community grew, the nuns of Cambrai also suffered serious setbacks before finding a stable home back in their native England. Though Dom Augustine's works had been cleared of error in 1633, his works were again questioned in 1655, raising suspicions as to the nuns' orthodoxy—though they were cleared once again. The monastery was also located in a disputed area that saw continued fighting between France and Spain, with all the attendant problems of war. More, the nuns' fortunes were largely invested among English royalists, which led to serious financial hardship when the parliamentary forces deposed and exe-cuted Charles I in 1649.

Despite all this, the community endured and continued with relative security until the French Revolution. In October of 1793, after several years of evading molestation by the revolutionaries, the community, along with the vicar (then-President of the Congrega-tion) Dom George Augustine Walker and his assistant Dom James Higginson, were arrested and taken to prison. Relatively safe but deprived of sanitation and living on little food, most of the nuns endured for a year and a half, while four died in the meantime.

In May of 1795, securing passports back to England, the nuns (now numbering only seventeen) returned to their homeland. Received with kindness, they took up the running of a school at Woolton, where they would educate young Catholic ladies. Eventually in 1835 (six years after the passing of the Roman Catholic Relief Act), the Stanbrook estate in Worcestershire was procured for the community and the nuns took up residence in 1838. Owing to cultural and prac-tical factors, strict enclosure was impossible throughout this time and would not be reinstated until 1880, through the tireless efforts of many parties. In the twentieth century the literary tradition of the community was taken forward by, for example, Dame Felicitas Corrigan (†2003) and Dame Maria Boulding (†2009). Their writ-ings include translations of the works of Saint Augustine, which provide a link back to the patristic author whom Dame Gertrude so admired and who had a notable influence on her thought and writing. In the late nineteenth and twentieth centuries, the abbey also contributed to the revitalization of the Roman liturgy and developed a fine printing press. In 2009 the community moved to Wass in the North York Moors National Park, where they had a new, eco-friendly monastery built and where they now enter on a new chapter in the monastery's history.

DAME GERTRUDE MORE: HER POEMS
AND COUNSELS ON PRAYER AND CONTEMPLATION

As we have seen, Dame Gertrude's brief life was lived in a forma-tive and tumultuous time in the history of the Church, the west, and the Benedictine order. Her courageous leading of other young

English women into exile on the continent and founding of a convent within the newly formed English Benedictine Congregation spearheaded a Benedictine community that endures to the present day. In her brief years she gave much to her community and developed a contemplative prayer life that embodied the perennial teaching of monastic life in the Church—that a life of sacrifice, a life dedicated to the performance of the liturgy, a life given over to quiet recollection of God with others will lead simultaneously to a share in 'Christ's sufferings' and his 'encouragement' (2 Cor 1:5), to the gift of contemplative union with God in this life and total enjoyment of eternal union in the life to come. In the poems, devotions, and counsels on prayer and contemplation that she penned during her lifetime, Dame Gertrude's is a confident voice calling out (sometimes forcefully) from the relative seclusion of the cloister.

As discussed briefly above, Dame Gertrude was formed by the spiritual teaching of Dom Augustine Baker. Much has been written elsewhere about Dom Augustine's teaching on the contemplative life. Given this, and that the present volume seeks to illuminate Dame Gertrude's understanding of the contemplative life, a thorough introduction to Dom Augustine's teaching will not be found here. However, Dom Augustine did much to help Dame Gertrude, so something must be said of his influence on her.

Dom Augustine had a storied career in England and on the continent, and after his own profession as a monk he too had difficulties with the Ignatian spirituality (especially its focus on sensual and imaginative discursive meditations and regular thorough examination of conscience) then common in the Latin Church. His first mystical experience occurred in 1608 and led to a profound depression. After several years engaged once again in worldly pursuits, he encountered a traditional monastic work on contemplation, which led to his complete dedication to contemplative prayer for the rest of his life. Though Dom Augustine developed his own schema for the life of prayer and stages of contemplation ('propensities'; the 'Divine Call'; the different sorts of prayer, including vocal prayer, discursive meditation, prayer of immediate acts, prayer of sensible affections, prayer of aridity), what was most important and pertinent in his teaching for Dame Gertrude and many others was that Dom Augustine 1. acknowledged that one way of prayer was not suitable for everyone alike; 2. encouraged each person to seek after the 'Divine Call' in their own life, in order to ascertain what way of prayer was best for that individual; 3. understood his role as superior and spiritual director as facilitating the growth of his pupils in the spiritual life rather than as protecting them by commanding them to do this or that; and 4. recognized that the Benedictine life was one oriented essentially toward contemplation. For many individuals this essential orientation was not supported by the kind of imaginative, discursive meditations and emphasis on examination of conscience so often prescribed for religious at the time. This last point is the culmination of the others and opened up Dame Gertrude's prayer life in ways she had not experienced before. Most especially, Dom Augustine's general avoidance of discursive meditation and his encouragement to listen to one's own 'Call' opened Dame Gertrude up to the perennial monastic tradition of formless, imageless contemplation that invites union with God's own simplicity through the soul's own simplicity.

While we might hunt through Dame Gertrude's poems and counsels for select terms and correspondences in order to lay out her 'system' of contemplation, this would be in ways beside the point. Theology for conceptual and doctrinal clarity is incumbent upon the Church, but there are also simply the depths of human experience and the direct encounter with the Living God that mystics struggle and strain to say something about, which in ways go beyond all conceptual frameworks. Though we might take Dame Gertrude's emphasis on the Divine Call and the voluntary abstraction from the senses leading to the soul's stark simplicity as a 'system', she was clearly not interested in the nuanced distinctions that many scholastic thinkers were. This is not to say that such thinkers, including such great doctors of the Church as Saint Bonaventure, Saint Thomas Aquinas, and, to a lesser extent, Dom Augustine Baker himself were not great mystics and contemplatives. But their projects of strict distinctions and clarity of conceptual frameworks were not Dame Gertrude's. As the French Benedictine Dom Henri Le Saux (1910–73; also known as Swami Abhishiktananda) says about his own probings of the heights of the mystical experience: 'God's inscrutability is not an intellectual concept, the apophatism of philosophy, but a personal experience in the Spirit of the depths of God'.[5] One of the mystical

---

[5]   Swami Abhishiktananda (Dom Henri Le Saux), *Saccidananda: A Christian Approach to Advaitic Experience* [1974] (Delhi: ISPCK, 1997), p. 3.

writers formative in Dame Gertrude's life (and a favorite of Dom Augustine Baker), Constantine Barbanson, expresses a similar idea when he asserts that the 'scholastic' ideal of contemplation, while valid, is too focused on the intellect. He sides with the 'mystic' way that focuses on the will's capacity—always aided by grace—to love God beyond all concepts and thought.[6] In this focus on practice and experience, Dame Gertrude finds greater accord with the earlier medieval and monastic tradition of Saint Gregory the Great and Saint Benedict himself, neither of whom define a *system* of contemplation but both of whom were clearly concerned with the primary place of contemplation in the Christian life.

After her premature death in 1633, someone entered Dame Gertrude's cell and discovered her personal papers. Though apparently not prepared for publication, the meditations, counsels, prayers, and poems Dame Gertrude had composed and compiled formed a treasure trove of contemplative wisdom. Dom Augustine Baker acquired the papers and began preparing them for printing, also incorporating some of the material into the *Life and Death of Dame Gertrude More* that he wrote shortly after her death. However, since, after he was moved to Douai, Dom Augustine was later moved back to England, it fell to Fr Francis Gascoigne (1605–76) to finalize the volume of Dame Gertrude's writings. He had it printed at Paris in 1658 as *Confessiones Amantis: The Spiritual Exercises of the Most Vertuous and Religious Dame Gertrude More* (hereafter '1658'). One manuscript in Oxford's Bodleian Library copied out in the seventeenth century (hereafter 'Rawlinson') contains the *Confessiones Amantis* and some of her poems. Aside from some of her miscellaneous devotional items incorporated into Dom Augustine's *The Holy Practices of a Deuine Lover, or the Sainctly Ideots Deuotions* (1657) (present also in two manuscripts) and extracts from the *Confessiones* in a few other scattered manuscripts, 1658 and Rawlinson contain all that we know of Dame Gertrude's works.[7]

---

[6]   See Constantin de Barbanson, *Les secrets sentiers de l'amour divin: esquels est cachée la vraye sapience céleste & le royaume de Dieu en nos ames* (Paris : Chez Desclée & Cie, 1932), II.15; Constantine Barbanson, *The Secret Paths of Divine Love*, trans. A Nun of Stanbrook Abbey (New York: Benziger Brothers, 1928), II.15.

[7]   For the extracts, see *Confessiones Amantis*, ix.

Dame Gertrude focuses her poems and counsels on the need for simplicity and humility in order to enter the heights of contemplation and mystical union with God through love. The most developed treatment of this view is found in her text called 'An Apology for Herself and Her Spiritual Guide and Director, the Venerable Augustine Baker' (hereafter, the 'Apology'). This work's primary purpose is to defend Dom Augustine Baker and his teaching. But because Dame Gertrude says specifically that the document is intended for her 'own private comfort and help, and to be seen by no other', to serve as 'a great help to me ... when I am either in obscurity of temptation or other bodily indisposition', it does not appear that this exact text is the testimony that she sent to the General Chapter of 1633 mentioned above. As it is the most substantial work among the texts gathered in this book, it can provide an anchor for understanding the rest of her works.

The 'Apology', throughout its length and various topics, revolves, spiral-like, between two poles. On the one hand, Dame Gertrude is concerned, echoing Saint Benedict's Rule itself (see for example RB Prol. 46, 39.1, 40.1–2), with something that seems self-evident to us moderns but needed saying in her own time, namely, that different people have different spiritual needs. Her insistence on this point makes clear that some perceived Dom Augustine to be teaching the nuns at Cambrai that they did not need to obey their properly assigned superiors and that they only needed to heed his own teaching. The 'Apology' begins by refuting this perception. In doing so it addresses the nuns' times for mental prayer and recollection, the nature of obedience itself, and the role of traditional monastic virtues (like humility) in cultivating love for God.

Most acute and extended is her treatment of obedience, which she asserts is the virtue without which no other virtue is pleasing to God, in traditional Benedictine fashion. Yet she qualifies this traditional assessment with an explicitly non-authoritarian interpretation. For Dame Gertrude, true obedience 'is an obedience that regardeth God and that doth what he would, and not a foolish pretended obedience which is in the letter and not in the spirit'. Dame Gertrude promotes the virtues of the monastic world, but she insists on their proper execution—blind adherence to superiors' commands is not actually obedience; assenting to superiors' commands in line with how the individual hears the Divine Call in their interior is. This is likely the riskiest and boldest contribution that Dame Gertrude makes to the monastic tradition she embodies so well. In her time and place—early modern Europe—such a perspective had to be explained and practised carefully, for it nuanced the nature of the Church's institutional authority. Without claiming any kind of complete or arbitrary freedom from the Church's or her congregation's hierarchies, Dame Gertrude courageously asserted that authority had to be exercised in the interest of the perfection of the human soul. She vehemently yearns for the spirit over the letter while recognizing legitimate authority in its proper sphere.

Less potentially fraught perhaps, Dame Gertrude grounds her observations on the virtues (especially obedience) and the practice of monastic life in the assertion that set, imaginative meditations and intense self-scrutiny (while apparently effective in the active life) are not typically helpful in the contemplative life. She reveals that, because her spiritual director failed to recognize the lack of help she received from discursive meditations and insisted, as her superior, that his preferences for her were intrinsically best suited to her development, for a long time she thought that there was something wrong with her. Once Dom Augustine showed her there was another way (the 'way of love', of simple tending toward God without images in silence or, at most, in short prayers of the will), she realized that the problem was not in herself but rather in a mismatch of practitioner and practice. With Dom Augustine's help she found a way that supported her inner life and led to its fruition. Ultimately, this first pole of the 'Apology' explains that contemplative prayer along the lines Dom Augustine recommended brought Dame Gertrude from the brink of desolation and despair in her monastic life to great fulfilment.

The other pole of the 'Apology' receives less treatment but is the upshot of all that Dame Gertrude underwent in the conflict surrounding authority in her community. This is her reflection on her unitive experience—Dame Gertrude's experience of union with God in the context of the monastic life's silence, obedience, humility, and love of God above all other loves. Her own teaching on the nature of contemplative union is summed up in the following passage from the 'Apology':

It sufficeth not for the soul that there is in God himself, whom the soul seeketh after, simplicity or unity. But there must also be all possible simplicity in the soul herself, for the making her fit to treat with God and thereupon become united to him. The more simple or one that the soul is (which is that the more she is free and rid of all thoughts of creatures which cause multiplicity), the liker is she to God who is simplicity itself, and the more apt and worthy to become united to him. And therefore, all the cunning and industry of a spiritual master should ever be by all lawful means to rid the soul of all multiplicity, incumbrances, blocks, and all other things that are enemies to the foresaid simplicity in soul. And indeed, every image of a created thing is an impediment to the said simplicity, and therefore is to be rejected at such time as the soul is in case to apply itself immediately to God.

For Dame Gertrude, as for the monastic tradition in which she swims, mystical union, the heights of contemplation, is not reserved for intellectuals or those with extraordinary gifts of visions or the like. Rather, 'as this simplicity is grounded upon plain and simple instructions, so is it and must it withal be, as well, founded upon simple and plain dealing with God and man—simply intending God and avoiding all double dealing and all undue intention'. Here she echoes the author of *The Cloud of Unknowing* in her insistence on the divine simplicity as well as the bare need for 'intending' God.[8] This resonance with the *Cloud*-author will likely not come as a surprise to some readers of Dame Gertrude's works, given Dom Augustine's interest in the medieval English mystics and the Cambrai nuns' pivotal role in copying key texts out for posterity. What might come as more of a surprise is the resonance her witness has to Saint Gregory the Great's teaching—though, given Saint Gregory's immense influence on the western Church in general, perhaps this should not surprise us at all. Gregory says much the same thing of mystical union as Dame Gertrude in his *Homilies on Ezekiel*:

> For often we wish to ponder the invisible nature of Almighty God but by no means avail, and the soul, wearied by the very

8   See *Cloud of Unknowing*, Chapter 3 and passim; *Cloud of Unknowing with the Book of Privy Counsel*, trans. by Carmen Acevedo Butcher (Boulder: Shambhala, 2009).

difficulties, withdraws into herself and makes for herself and from herself the steps of her ascent ... But our mind, if spread out in carnal images, by no means suffices to consider itself or the nature of the soul because it is led by as many thoughts as it is, so to speak, blinded by obstacles ... Then the first step is to compose oneself, the second to see the like of this composure, the third to rise above oneself and by intention submit to the contemplation of the invisible Creator. But one by no means composes himself unless he has first learned to curb the apparitions of earthly and heavenly images from his mind's eye and cast out and tread down whatever of sight, hearing, smell, touch, and taste occurs to his bodily thought, in order that he may inwardly seek such as is free thereof ... Then all things are to be driven away by the hand of discernment from the mind's eye so that the soul may regard herself as she was created, above the body but below God ... When therefore the soul thinks of herself without bodily images she has already entered the first door. But this door leads on to the other in order that something from the nature of Almighty God may be contemplated ... But the very consideration and discernment thereof is already to enter to some extent, because from her appraisement the soul gathers what she perceives of the uncircumscribed Spirit which incomprehensibly rules those things which He incomprehensibly created ... And the One makes all but is not divided in all. For He is truly the Highest and never unlike Himself. But the soul, although she is never diverse by nature, yet is diverse through thought.[9]

For Gregory, God is simple ('never unlike Himself'), never diverse. The soul too is simple in its very nature, but through thought and sense impressions it becomes diverse. The key to contemplative vision for Gregory is to withdraw from bodily sensations, then 'earthly and heavenly images', so that the soul may 'regard itself as she was created'. Discernment of this simplicity leads, with grace, to a glimpse of the 'uncircumscribed Spirit' through a reestablished mutual harmony in that simplicity. Though the terms change, the similarity between Gregory's and Gertrude's emphasis on the

---

[9] Gregory the Great, *Homilies on the Book of the Prophet Ezekiel*, trans. Theodosia Tomkinson (Etna, CA: Center for Traditionalist Orthodox Studies, 2008), II.5.8–10, pp. 339–41.

experience of interiority, gradual abstraction from sense and image, and simplicity of soul according with the simplicity of God is unmistakable. When attention is on the lived experience of contemplative union, only so many basic moves come to the fore.

In her emphasis on simplicity and complete guilelessness, she also echoes other monastic teachers who similarly avoided complex systems and subtleties. Another resonant example is the apex of Saint Romuald's († c. 1025) *Brief Rule*: 'Empty yourself and sit waiting, content with the grace of God'. Emptying oneself of multiplicity and waiting for the Divine Call are the means Dame Gertrude teaches are most important for contemplative union with God. And though she spends much less time in the 'Apology' with this pole, these means are precisely why the other pole (concerning authority, obedience, and the politics of orders in the Catholic Reformation Church) are so important—if people are not able to make time and space for this internal disposition due to their superiors' demands, the ultimate purpose of the religious life (and all human life), that is, contemplative union with the Triune God, will be all the more difficult to realize. She puts greater effort into assessing the mundane aspects of the religious life, but this is precisely because without these in proper order, the more essential and contemplative aspects of the religious life are not likely to flourish.

Before moving to the other texts collected here, a word should be said about practice. More so than many earlier monastic discussions of prayer, Dame Gertrude's 'Apology' offers the reader something on the *practice* of contemplative prayer. In her reckoning of the contemplative life, the simplicity of the soul (which will accord in unity with the simplicity of God) is arrived at through the laying aside of all images and inordinate affections for any and all creatures. When first setting out on this 'exercise of the will', the aspirant needs simply to enter regularly into 'mental prayer' (by which she means silent recollection or what we late-moderns sometimes call 'contemplative prayer') rather than striving by force to root out all 'imperfections' before putting 'out into deep water' (Luke 5:4). As the habit of mental prayer is sincerely developed, either imperfections will drop off of their own accord or this self-abnegation will produce fruit from remaining imperfections through the growth of humility.

This habit of mental prayer is strengthened through periods of the day set aside especially for the purpose. When Dame Gertrude discusses the periods of mental prayer that the nuns at Cambrai observed each day, we find out several interesting things. Since the habit had to be developed, Dom Augustine had insisted on 'the necessity of prosecuting it daily and diligently too, if they desired to arrive to any perfect degree in the love of God'. Such prayer needs to be practised daily, twice a day (morning and evening), to establish regularity, since 'it may be practised by some a long time before they find any extraordinary benefit by it, and till they find the effect of it in their own souls they may be apt to neglect and make no esteem of it'. Dame Gertrude suggests that 'at first for four or five years' such regularity is necessary, but after that this strictness of schedule might be loosened. In these periods, and then infused throughout the day as such mental prayer becomes a well-established habit, ultimately the aspirant 'must give all to God, without any reservation wittingly and willingly of any inordinate affection to any creature'. As this habitual awareness continues to establish the soul in 'tending towards God by the exercise of the will, … prosecuted together with true mortification', the soul will be brought 'to a mystical union and perfection in time convenient'. Simplicity itself, but an existential challenge to the prideful and selfish tendencies of the soul without the aid of grace and discipline.

The other counsels on prayer and contemplation found in Dame Gertrude's papers after her death reiterate key aspects laid out in the 'Apology'. In fact, much of the material in the longer tracts is taken from the 'Apology' itself, reframed to accentuate particular points made in the larger work. Though somewhat repetitive, I have retained them in the present volume for completeness and also to show the adaptability of Dame Gertrude's thought—she clearly considered some of her points salient enough to stand on their own in isolation from her more complex and sprawling work. Somewhat ironically, the short texts 'The Simple Exercise of the Will' and 'A Poesy' might have the greater force for being so stripped down and direct. Especially the former strikes a similar tone to much of the directness and sincerity of *The Cloud of Unknowing* and *The Book of Privy Counsel*.

Dame Gertrude's poems are, paradoxically, interesting in their very plainness. Unlike her contemporaries and near-contemporaries Robert Southwell (†1595), John Donne (1572–1631), George Herbert (1593–1633), Richard Crashaw (1613–49), and others, Dame Gertrude did not seek to push the limits of poetic form nor to practise a 'high style' of verse. In the main, she uses as her basic form what is called 'common metre' (the name expresses well how little novelty is implied in its use). Common metre comprises four lines per stanza, alternating one iambic tetrameter (four-beat or eight-syllable line) with one iambic trimeter (three-beat or six-syllable line) twice, with the second and the fourth lines rhyming a-b-c-b. Her longer poems are set explicitly in 'common-metre double', which is comprised of two sets of common metre quatrains made into one stanza. She also uses this stanza structure to special effect in a few poems and employs heroic couplets (rhyming pairs of iambic pentameter—five-beat or ten-syllable lines) in one poem. As in metre, so in poetic figures. The poetic pyrotechnics of metaphysical verse and the high styles that flourished in Dame Gertrude's age (Spenser's *Faerie Queen* had been published in 1590–6; Shakespeare's sonnets had been published in 1609; and Milton first published *Paradise Lost* in 1667) were not for her. Dame Gertrude employed a plain style, with minimal imagery and use of metaphor and simile. All this lends a consistently homely and humble air to her poems.

While we might dismiss her poems, then, as unworthy of sustained attention, as paling in comparison to her contemporaries, if looked at through a Benedictine lens, her strategies are not so surprising and are, in fact, quite skillful. Saint Benedict in his Rule is of course concerned for the restraint and proper use of speech 'out of esteem for silence', and since 'In a flood of words you will not avoid sin'.[10] As Jaime Goodrich has recently shown, various texts from Cambrai demonstrate that the nuns applied the Benedictine preference for restraint of speech to their own works in prose and verse.[11] Basically, the use of a 'low' or 'plain' style supported an atmosphere of humility.

While Dame Gertrude surely agreed with this rationale for a plain style, an observation in her 'Apology' takes this further into the very nature of the contemplative life and of the soul:

> All that draws to multiplicity and estranging from God in our interior let us bless ourselves from as the poison of our soul, and any thing or creature that would interpose itself between

---

10   RB 6.2 and 6.4. See also RB 6 and RB 7.56–8 and 7.60–1.
11   See Goodrich, 'Low & Plain Stile'.

God and our soul is an impediment to contemplation. Woe be to those souls, if they have the capacity for an internal life, that are studying how to write and speak to creatures to the pouring out of their affections. For by this means their affection will be taken up by the way, and the creatures will be more regarded than the Creator, though the subject of their writings be of and for God. Much vanity I have known in this kind, the ghostly father admiring the wit, devotion, and humility of his penitent. And the penitent, by having her proceedings in that kind admired, published, and applauded by her ghostly father, was in great danger to vanish away in her own cogitations. These sensible proceedings often draw the soul (do what she can) more to men than God.

Here Dame Gertrude clearly asserts that learning to write and speak in ways that pour out one's affections with elaborate style not only leads to pride or vainglory but also to 'multiplicity'. As we have seen above, Dame Gertrude's way of love, in the stream of western monastic views of the contemplative life more generally, insists that 'multiplicity' in the soul distracts from the soul's tending toward God, since God is simple. In this tendency toward multiplicity in the formal and figural complexities of high style writing, she sees its artifice and genius as unconducive (what she might call 'a stop') to the contemplative life. A staid and straightforward poetry, on the other hand, trains the imagination and soul squarely on God himself. A form of self-abnegation, the soul in this poetics has no other quarter in which to distract itself.

In this vein, her poems explore her interior world and at times move outward (to the communion of saints), but not to shock her audience with creative genius or novelty. Rather, her poems incessantly focus the soul intent on God upon the 'one thing necessary' (Luke 10:42). Whether or not we agree with how Dame Gertrude views the relationship of poetics to contemplation, the integrity of her view in light of Benedictine principles stands. This being said, the subtlety with which Dame Gertrude tracks the movements of her will and the oscillation between faithfulness and falling short of the mark in her poems are executed with dexterity. The plain style she employs only makes the moments of rhetorical flourish and simile she does allow herself the more arresting. In these poems, Dame Gertrude allows herself more leeway to witness directly to the movements of her soul, to her intuition of the ways God plays with her and loves her, than she does in her prose writing, as seems fitting. Throughout the poems, she exhorts and observes, laying out her understanding of the monastic life and contemplation in supple rumination, and in ways directly corresponding to the themes in her prose works. In her humble but sturdy idiom, Dame Gertrude can still surprise us with a turn of phrase or an acute insight into the psychology of the spiritual life. Even after centuries, the perceptive tracing out of the love affair between God and the soul that her poems offer impresses, so long as we are not looking for consistent dramatic intensity and formal fireworks.

In her straightforward and clear emphasis on the soul's simplicity leading to intimacy and union with God's simplicity, Dame Gertrude clearly sets forth a perennial touchstone of the western monastic and contemplative tradition, which in its way makes her teaching the less remarkable. What makes her teaching all the more remarkable and valuable, however, is her acute pragmatism and straightforwardness when discussing the depths of contemplative experience and that she was a seventeenth-century cloistered nun. That a young woman writing in the vernacular in the early-modern period from 'behind the grate' could articulate so precisely and simply the coincidence of the accumulated experience of the western monastic tradition and her own lived experience is a testament to that tradition's enduring validity as well as her own authority. In this validity and authority, we find Dame Gertrude's a Christian, monastic, contemplative voice well worth tending to.

The Edition

I have attempted to maintain Dame Gertrude More's own language as much as possible in the present edition. However, for ease of reading for non-specialist audiences, Gracewing and I have agreed that updating the spelling and punctuation to accord with modern usage was desirable. That said, in not having altered her actual words to make sentences shorter or more straightforward in syntax (except in rare occasions marked by brackets), plenty of the present texts' sentences would be considered unwieldy at best by modern prose standards. But, again, to be as true as possible to her seventeenth-century manner of writing and way of thinking, we have thought it best to retain her actual wording, phrases, and clauses.

As will be seen, 1658 included editorial manicules in the margin, which I have retained.

In the prose works and a few of the poems ('O Glorious Saint, Whose Heart did Burn' and 'To Our Most Holy Father Saint Benedict'), I have only had 1658 to work with and, in the case of 'O Lord my God', only Rawlinson. However, some of the poems are in both, so in those cases I have had to choose a source text. The versions do not differ drastically in content, but many single words have variants and sometimes entire lines find different expression. The modern editor of Dame Gertude's works, John Clark, has admitted that neither text is inherently superior or clearly what Dame Gertrude originally wrote. Since it was an aspect of the reading communities at Cambrai and surrounding religious houses to produce and copy works collaboratively in manuscript, and given that 1658 was mediated through at least two different male hands (Dom Augustine Baker and Fr Francis Gascoigne), I have opted to prefer Rawlinson's text for the present book. All variants can be found in the reprinted edition of 1658 by Marotti along with the scholarly edition by Clark (see 'Further Reading'). Because the present volume is intended for non-specialist audiences, I have decided against including apparatus that provides all the variants, which would clutter the page and render the experience of reading Dame Gertrude's poems and counsels less immediate. Hopefully, deferring to the hand-copied text circulating in the monasteries in the seventeenth-century English Benedictine houses will be seen by the reader as excusing any shortcomings in not providing both texts. I have followed the general order of Rawlinson and 1658 in the presentation of the respective works, but where works overlap in different order between the two versions and where works do not appear in both I have had simply to make choices on how to order them. When working with manuscripts and early printed books, such decisions have to be made, and there are no perfect or natural choices. I hope Dame Gertrude would be happy with how I have chosen to present her works here.

Poems

My God to Thee I Dedicate [1]

Y GOD, to thee I dedicate
    this simple work of mine,
and with it also heart and soul
    to be forever thine.
No other motive I will have
    but by it thee to praise
and to stir up my frozen soul
    by love itself to raise. [2]

All things, desires, and loves are vain
    but only that which tends
to God alone, our chiefest good
    and all things else transcends.
My soul therefore by this sweet love
    shall day and night aspire
and rest in God all things above –
    my love and life's desire.

And while I live I'll never cease
    to languish for his love,
breathing and sighing after him
    till he my life remove.
For since I live not where I love,
    how can I comfort find,
but only in your song of love
    by love to me assigned?

---

[1]   In Rawlinson this poem begins the work Dame Gertrude calls *Amor ordinem nescit* (*Love Knows No Order*, which Dom Augustine Baker and Fr Francis Gascoigne called *Confessiones Amantis*), apparently serving as a dedication for the larger work. Whether this was her own intent or the choice of the manuscript's scribe is difficult to know, especially since parts of this poem are found throughout 1658, rather than at its beginning.

[2]   From 'My God, to thee I dedicate' to 'by love itself to raise' is found among the devotions gathered after *Amor ordinem nescit* in 1658.

In whatsoe'er this word[3] is writ
    it yields a silver sound,
but if this word I miss in it
    methinks I want my ground.
Nothing so simple can be penned,
    if it but treat of love
but that it serveth in some sort
    my mis'ry to remove.

And shall my soul by senseless love,
    which yet was never true,
have giv'n more love where it was lost
    than where it's only due?
O no, my God, but rather let
    this folly be to me
a means to urge my sinful soul
    to love more fervently.

And henceforth let me draw no breath
    but to aspire by love
to thee, my God and all my good
    by whom I live and move.
No stag in chase so thirsty is
    or greedy of sweet spring,
as is my soul of thee, my God,
    whilst here I sighing sing.[4]

My soul, where is thy love and Lord,
    since him thou canst not find?
O cheer up, heart, be comforted –
    for he is in thy mind.
To him relation one may have
    as often as he goes

---

3   That is, 'love'.
4   See Ps 42:1.

into the closet of his heart
his griefs for to disclose.[5]

As silly lambs from rav'ning wolves
for help to shepherds fly,
so shall my soul in ev'ry case
for help and counsel hie
to thee, my God, by humble prayer
in hope and confidence,
that thou, my Lord, wilt succour me
and be my soul's defence.

For seeing that my God is rich,
how can I say I'm poor?
He is more mine than I my own –
what can I wish for more?
And in his majesty and pow'r
much more I will rejoice
than if of all in heav'n and earth
I had command and choice.[6]

O I desire no tongue nor pen
but to extol his praise,
in which excess I'll melt away
ten thousand thousand ways.
And as one that is sick with love
ingrafts in ev'ry tree
the names and praise of them they love,
so shall it be with me.[7]

---

[5] See Matt 6:6.
[6] From 'All things, desires, and loves are vain' to 'I had command and choice' is found in the seventh confession of *Amor ordinem nescit* in 1658. See also the third to last paragraph of the 'Apology' and the first paragraph of 'The Interior or Spiritual Disposition'.
[7] From 'O I desire no tongue nor pen' to 'so shall it be with me' is found among the devotions gathered after *Amor ordinem nescit* in 1658.

Which to attempt, if it seem much
    to those that it espy,
saying, 'tis only for the just
    to thee for help to fly,
what then becomes of sinners poor?
    or to whom shall they go
if not to thee? Ah, pity us,
    for we may love also.

Jesus did publicans receive,
    nor yet did he disdain
harlots and thieves that beggèd help.
    Since which, who can complain
or fear that he will them reject
    when they their sins repent
and fly unto his mercy sweet,
    whose heart doth soon relent?

when we with tears beseech him to
    forgive our sins so many
and give such grace and strength henceforth
    as not to yield to any?
My God, one thing alone thou know'st
    I fear and apprehend,
which is my Lord for to displease,
    whose mercies have no end.

From all that doth displease thy eyes,
    be pleased to set me free.
For nothing else in heav'n or earth
    do I desire but thee.
And let me rather death embrace
    than thee, my God, offend,
or in my heart to leave a place
    for any other friend.[8]

---

[8] From 'And let me rather death embrace' to 'for any other friend' is appended
    to the end of *Amor ordinem nescit* in Rawlinson, with 'O' for 'And' and 'before

Nothing would grieve my soul so much
    as in me to perceive
that the affection to the world
    should me of thine bereave.
I know thou must possess alone,
    or else we are not thine –
in manner such as we should be
    if light to us do shine

as thou desirest it should do
    by grace within our hearts.
And all the helps that thou hast giv'n
    and daily yet impart
to us, intended were by thee,
    that we might live alone
to thee, our God, who fills pure souls
    with joys that are unknown.

And woe to them a thousand times
    who interest have in any
or have divided hearts to thee
    after thy gifts so many.
For thou hast purchasèd our love
    at too, too dear a rate
to have a partner in our heart,
    which justly thou dost hate.

O this thy wrong makes angels blush;
    O make it far from me.
Since I am both body and soul
    consecrated to thee.
And I will also grieve with them
    to see thee have such wrong
from souls called out by thee thyself
    to sing with them the song

I thee' for 'than thee, my God'.

7

of love and praise to thee our God,
    and even in this place
thee to contemplate in our manner —
    O sweet and happy grace.
If we would die unto ourselves
    and all things else but thee,
it would be natural to our souls
    for to ascend and be

united to our Center dear,
    to which our soul would hie,
being as proper then for us
    as fire upwards to fly.
O let us therefore love my God,
    for love pertains to him,
and let our souls seek nothing else
    but in this love to swim.

Till we, absorbed by his sweet love,
    return from whence we came,
where we shall melt into that love
    which joyeth me to name.
And never can I it too much
    speak of or it desire,
since that my God, who's Love itself,
    doth only love require.

Come, therefore, all, and let us love
    and with a pure aspect
regard our God in all we do
    and he will us protect.
O that all things upon the earth
    echoèd with thy praise,
my everlasting glorious God,
    the Ancient of days.

And I do wish with all my soul
    perpetually to sing,

but seeing this I cannot do
    my sighs to heav'n shall ring.
Yea, if I writ out all the sea,
    yet can I not express
the joy and comfort I do feel
    in what thou dost possess.

No gifts or grace or comfort here,
    how great soe'er they be,
can satiate my longing soul
    whilst I possess not thee.
For thou art all my heart's desire,
    yea, all that I do crave
in heav'n or earth, yea, now or ever
    th'art all my soul would have.

And I do wish with all my soul
    that to thee I could pray
with all my heart and all my strength[9]
    ten-thousand times a day.
Let peoples, tribes, and tongues confess
    unto thy majesty.[10]
And let us never cease to sing
    Sanctus, Sanctus![11] to thee,[12]

who be adored by ancients all,
    whose crowns lie at thy feet,[13]
as justice doth require they should
    and as it is most meet.
And we, invited by thy saints

---

[9]   Cf. Deut 6:5, Matt 22:37, Mark 12:30 and 33, and Luke 10:27.
[10] See Rev 7:9.
[11] 'Holy, holy!'; referring to the *Sanctus* of the Mass and its biblical source, the prophet's vision of seraphim singing to the divine majesty in Isa 6:3 and the four living creatures singing to the same in Rev 4:8.
[12] From 'my God, one thing alone thou know'st' to 'Sanctus, Sanctus! to thee' is found in the seventh confession of *Amor ordinem nescit* in 1658.
[13] See Rev 4:10.

and angels thee to praise,
will join with them with voices high
    our souls by love to raise

to thee, of whom I'll never crave,
    whilst this my soul hath breath,
but that I may united be
    to thee in life and death.
My God, my love and very life,
    my glory and my crown,
my light shall only tend to this:
    to joy in thy renown.

O let me, as the silver streams
    into the ocean glide,
melt into that vast sea of love
    which into thee doth slide!
The little birds do chirp and sing
    and never weary be
of praising my creator dear,
    and I scarce think on thee.

But what I cannot by myself
    accomplish in this kind,
I'll beg of thy celestial court
    who to this is assigned
by thy all-living, loving self,
    to whom all love is due,
to whom my heart hath been most false
    or, rather, never true.

The which rememb'ring, my poor soul
    doth even fail and faint
as any would that here should find
    me out, my sins to paint.
But thou thyself dost say to us
    thou wilt not sinner's death,

but that we do convert and live[14]
ev'n while our souls have breath.

And no more than to cease to be,
    no more canst thou refuse
to pardon humble penitents
    that do themselves accuse.
Being no person thou excepts,
    all having cost thee dear –
yea, even thy [own] life itself –
    how can I therefore fear?

If ever yet thou hadst disdained
    sinners that fled to thee,
then had I little cause of hope
    but this none yet did see.
For if they do return to thee,
    thy heart thou wilt not close,
as witness can my wretched soul
    that was so like to lose

all grace and goodness (if thou hadst
    not with thy help prevented)
by sins that would by bloody tears
    be while I live lamented,
if I as grateful were to thee
    as thou deserv'st I should,
or as another in my case
    unto thy mercy would.

And all that time thou livedst here,
    thou many ways did shew
that none should be refused by thee
    who didst with mercy flow.
And this my wicked heart did find,
    who after sins so many

---

[14]   See Ezek 18:23, 18:32, and 33:11 and 2 Pet 3:9.

have found much favour in thy eyes
    without deserving any.

O blessèd ever be my God
    for this preventing grace,
which I unworthy have received
    in this most happy place.[15]
I fled from thee by many sins
    and thou didst follow me
as if my mis'ry would have caused
    some detriment to thee.

How can this chase but wound my heart
    when I remember it,
and ever serve to humble me
    whilst at thy feet I sit?[16]
From whence, my Lord, my God, my all,
    permit me not to rise
till I do love thee as thou would'st,
    the which doth all comprise.[17]

For as thou know'st, all other loves
    but thine I do defy.
And let this love by thy sweet grace
    possess me totally.
All others for thy sake I love
    with equal charity.
Only where obligation claims
    justly more love for thee

to those that most advanced my love
    and my desire of thee,

---

[15]   That is, the Abbey of Our Lady of Comfort at Cambrai.
[16]   See Luke 10:39; Mary of Bethany sitting at the feet of Jesus as Martha serves
     is a traditional image for the contemplative life.
[17]   From 'But thou thyself dost say to us' to 'the which doth all comprise' is found
     in 'An Act of Contrition, Partly Taken Out of the Words of Blessed Saint
     Augustine' found after the poems gathered in 1658.

these by respect thou dost exact
    should be esteemed by me.
Yet not so much as to forget
    or weaken this thy love,
which by thy Law and will most just
    I should prefer above

them, which were but thy instruments.
    And, therefore, it would seem
very absurd if I should them
    more than thyself esteem,
who didst by them thy counsel give,
    which was so good for me,
and second it with thy sweet grace —
    the glory be to thee.
                        Amen.

Of Suffering and Bearing the Cross

OH, can that soul that loves her God
　　for very shame complain
to any other than himself
　　of what she doth sustain?
No way to him was ever found
　　or ever shall there be
but taking up thy Cross, my Lord,
　　thereby to follow thee.

This is the way, the truth, the life[18]
　　which leadeth unto heaven;
none is secure but only this
　　though it seem ne'er so even.
Those that do walk this happy path
　　Jesus doth company,
but those that go another way
　　will err most shamefully.

In this way do not think it much
　　if thou dost here endure
suff'ring, even by saints themselves;
　　for God doth this procure
that thou may'st seek himself alone
　　and put thy trust in him
and not in any creature living,
　　how good soe'er they seem.

For suff'ring by the means of ill
　　would little thee advance,
but to be censured by the good
　　goes near to thee, perchance.
Alas, we shew but little love,

---

[18]　See John 14:6.

if we must choose which way
our Lord shall try our love to him
and not in all obey.

We must submit ourselves to him
and be of cheerful heart,
for he expecteth much of her
that he gives Mary's part.[19]
For she must bear a censure hard
from all without exception.
Yet thou, O Lord, wilt her excuse,
who art her soul's election.

If she will patiently sustain
and be to thee attent,
thou fav'rably wilt judge of her
who knows her heart's intent.
For all but thee, as well she sees,
may err concerning her.
They only judge as they conceive,
but thou dost see most far.

Complain not therefore, loving soul,
if thou wilt be of those
who love their God more than themselves
and Mary's part have chose.
If all thou dost be taken ill
by those of high perfection,
and, farther, if thou be accus'd
to be of some great faction

---

[19] See Luke 10:38–42. Western tradition held from at least the time of Saint Gregory the Great that Saint Mary Magdalene, Mary of Bethany, and the sinner of Luke 7:36–50 were all the same woman. Contemplative authors throughout the centuries used Christ's remarks to Mary and Martha in Luke 10:38–42 as commentary on the nature of the contemplative and active lives. In the sixteenth century, the conflation of these three Gospel characters began to be questioned, but the traditional association endures to this day.

our Lord will answer for thee, if
    thou wilt but hold thy peace,
and if that he do think it good.
    If not content, surcease.
Leave all thy care to this thy God
    and him alone attend.
Yet what is ill reform in thee,
    and this will all amend

as far as he doth think it good,
    who is most just and wise,
for by afflictions he doth purge
    what doth displease his eyes.
Wilt thou, of all that lov'st thy God,
    from suff'ring be exempt?
O no, but bless (as others do)
    thy God and be content.

Amidst the several accidents
    that do to thee befall,
commit thyself and all to God
    who seeks our good in all.
Thyself art blind and canst not judge
    what is the best for thee,
but he doth pierce into all things
    how hidd'n soe'er they be.

My heart shall only this desire:
    that thou, my Lord, dispose
of all things as thou pleasest best
    till these my eyes thou close
by death, which I so much desire,
    because it will procure
me to enjoy my God, my all,
    where I shall be secure

that none from me can take my Lord,
    but for eternity

I shall enjoy my only good
  and to him ever be
united by a perfect love
  which none can interpose,
being by thee assurèd then
  that him I cannot lose.

O happy hour, when wilt thou come
  and set my spirit free,
that I may love and praise my God
  with all perpetually,
contemplating his glorious face
  with all that him adore,
singing with them his sweetest praise
  for ever, ever more?[20]

My God the *summum bonum*[21] is,
  yea, all that's good is his.
And those that seek himself alone
  of him shall never miss.
In thee, my God, my soul shall rest,
  not in created things.
For thou alone, O Lord of Lords,
  true peace to spirit brings.

All other things wished or desired,
  how good soe'er they be,
cause perturbation to our heart,
  nor can we rest in thee
whilst we do pleasure take in them
  contrary to thy mind,
and nothing prospers we attempt
  whilst we remain thus blind.

---

20 From 'Oh, can that soul that loves her God' to 'for ever, ever more' is inserted
    (with a number of variants) into the first confession of *Amor ordinem nescit*
    in 1658.
21 'highest good'

O God, the portion of my heart
be thou, my Lord, for ever.
In thee alone let me have part
and let no thing us sever.
I do invite with all my soul
all creatures thee to praise
and beg of thy celestial host
to supply our delays.

But praise thyself, my blessèd God,
yea, for them all and me,
for thou alone canst give what's due
unto thy majesty.

To Our Blessed Lady,
the Advocate of Sinners

ALL HAIL, O Virgin crowned with stars,
    and moon under thy feet:
obtain us pardon of our sins
    of Christ our Saviour sweet.
For though thou'rt Mother of my God,
    yet thy humility
disdaineth not this simple wretch
    that flies for help to thee.

Thou know'st thou art more dear to me
    than any can express
and that I do congratulate
    with joy thy happiness.
Thou, who art Queen of Heav'n and Earth,
    thy helping hand me lend,
that I may love and praise my God
    and have a happy end.

And though my sins me terrify,
    yet, hoping still in thee,
I find my soul refreshèd much
    when to thee I do [flee].
For thou most willingly to God
    petitions dost present
and dost obtain much grace for us
    in this our banishment.

The honour and the glorious praise
    by all be given thee,
which Jesus, thy beloved Son,
    ordained eternally
for thee, whom he exalts in heav'n
    above the angels all

and whom we sinners find a Mother
when unto thee we call.

O Mater Dei, memento mei.[22]
Amen.

As also my good angel, Saint Joseph, Saint John [the] Evangelist, Saint Martin, Saint Augustine, Saint Thomas of Aquino, and thou, my most holy father Saint Benedict.[23]

To Our Most Holy Father Saint Benedict

MOST GLORIOUS FATHER,
in whose school[24]
   I live and hope to die:
God grant I may observe thy Rule,
   for in that all doth lie.
For no perfection can be named
   which us it doth not teach.
O happy she who in her soul
   the sense thereof doth reach!
But many praise obedience
   and thy humility,
and yet conceive not as they should
   what either of them be.
The simple, humble, loving souls
   only the sense find out
of any discreet, obedient Rule,
   and these are void of doubt.
Yea, under shadow of thy wings
   they up to heaven fly
and taste here in this vale of tears
   what perfect peace doth lie
hid in performance of thy Rule
   that leadeth unto heaven.
O happy souls who it perform,
   the ways so sweet and even!
By prayer and patience it's fulfilled,
   charity, obedience –
by seeking after God alone
   and giving none offence.
The more I look upon thy Rule,
   the more in it I find.

---

[24]   See RB Prol.45.

O do to me the sense unfold
   for letter makes us blind!
And blessèd, yea, a thousand times
   be thou who it hast writ,
and thy sweet blessing give to them
   who truly perform it.
For those are they which will conserve
   this house in perfect peace,
without which all we do is lost,
   and all that's good will cease.
And praisèd be our glorious God,
   who gave to thee such grace –
not only him thyself to seek
   but also out to trace
a way so easy and secure
   (if we will but thee hear)
to have relation to our God,
   who is to us so near.
For at this thou dost chiefly aim:
   that God our souls do teach.
O if we did truly obey,
   he would by all things preach
his will to us by ev'ry thing
   that did to us befall.
And then, as thou desir'st it should,
   he would be *all in all*.[25]
O pray, dear father, that he ever be
   our only love and all eternally. *Amen.*

Saint Scholastica, Saint Gertrude, and, in fine, all in heaven or on earth that are pleasing to thee, be pleased to make me partaker of their merits and prayers. And above all, wash me in thy Precious Blood, one drop whereof had been sufficient to have redeemed a thousand worlds. In this is my hope and confidence, by this I hope to be enriched with all that is wanting in me.

[25]   See 1 Cor 15:28.

For, in that thou art and possessest, I more rejoice and exult than if I had whatsoever on earth or in heaven I could desire at my command. In this joy I cry out with all my heart, with all my soul, and with all my strength:[26]

O how much good and happiness do I possess, seeing my God (who is more myself than I myself am) doth possess so infinite glory, majesty, and so infinite good things. For indeed I have and hold him more mine own than any thing that ever I had or held heretofore. This is the comfort of my poverty and the repose of my labour. This my most delightful, most amiable, most bright and beautiful and most glorious God is always present with me, to hear my praises and receive my petitions. In him I am rich, though in myself I am poor and contemptable. To him my most loving God, be given now and ever all laud and praise and glory, by all in heaven and earth, for ever and ever. Amen.

---

[26]   Cf. Deut 6:5, Matt 22:37, Mark 12:30 and 33, and Luke 10:27.

O Glorious Saint, Whose Heart did Burn[27]

for Saint Augustine

O GLORIOUS SAINT, whose heart did
burn
and flame with love divine:
remember me, most sinful wretch,
who hunger-starved doth pine
for want of that which thou enjoy'st
in such abundant measure –
it is my God that I do mean,
my joy and all my treasure.
Thy words, O saint, are truly sweet,
because thou dost address
them unto him who's only meet
our mis'ries to redress.

---

27   This poem is inserted into the end of the first confession of *Amor ordinem nescit* in 1658.

24

O Lord my God [28]

LORD MY GOD, to thee I do aspire,
    and only thee in soul do I desire.
No gift or grace, how good soe'er it be,
    can satiate her who nothing seeks but
    thee.

---

[28] This poem is found at the beginning of the thirty-eighth confession of *Amor ordinem nescit* in Rawlinson.

'A Litany in Homely Verse'

 FROM MULTIPLICITY and dejection,
that would breed our souls' confusion,
defend us, Lord, with thy benediction.

'Her Heart's Versicle'

as set at the front of her breviary

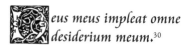 *eus meus impleat omne
desiderium meum.*[30]

For none but he
can satiate me.

In heart where love is seated
nothing but love is treated.

---

29   Texts gathered and modernized from *The Life and Death of Dame Gertrude More*, 245 and 265.
30   'May my God fulfil my every longing'.

26

Counsels

on

Prayer

and

Contemplation

An Apology for Herself

and Her Spiritual Guide and Director, the Venerable Augustine Baker

T MAY SEEM VERY STRANGE (and that very justly) that I should write what here I have written. But when I have here declared my reason for it, I may perhaps pass with the censure only of being a little presump-tuous. Yet God (who is my witness in all and my desire above all) knoweth upon what grounds I have done it and that it is but for my own private comfort and help and to be seen by no other but against my will, my superiors only excepted. From whom (as they shall require) I will not conceal the very secrets of my heart, much less this which I have written to lie by me, wherein there may be what they may mislike and correct, to which I shall most willingly submit myself. Yea, and though it seem to me to be a great help to me to have that which I have writ in more light to read when I am either in obscurity of temptation or other bodily indisposition to which I may be often incident, yet I will suppress it at their command and good pleasure, and put the want thereof willingly to the hazard – out of confidence in the assistance of God, who is a lover and rewarder of obedience, which virtue (howsoever it may be otherwise thought) I honour from my heart and believe verily that nothing that I do which doth not partake of that is of any regard at all with God.

This I have thus affirmed, because he who hath been my Master and Father in a spiritual life,[1] and hath brought me into a course which much satisfieth my soul and conscience between me and God (it tending to nothing but to love God

---

[1]   Dom Augustine Baker.

29

by seeking him above all graces and gifts, and by withdrawing all inordinate affection from all created things to become free to love and praise God in as pure and perfect a manner as this life will admit, and also to true submission and subjection of myself for God to whomsoever he puts over me in this life, with as great a contempt of myself as my frailty can reach unto) is, notwithstanding, taxed now by the same words in a manner which were alleged against our blessed Saviour: 'We have found this man subverting the people, and forbidding to give tribute to Caesar'.[2] Which, though none can justly say of him, yet it hath pleased God to honour him so much as to have him even in a public instrument[3] (which I have heard read) covertly pointed at, taxed, and accused of this manner of proceeding, they taking for their ground the imperfections of some through mere frailty committed in this kind. As also because some, who are of other ways and understand not this, affirm it may be inferred out of his books that subjects (in what they pretend to have a Divine Call to) may resist, con-tradict, and disobey superiors. Which, that it may be inferred I cannot deny, since a meaner wit than he that affirmeth this may draw strange consequences out of any book in the house, if he will look upon them with no other intention but to carp. But if they will take one place with another and consider what we believe, and practise also, according to our imperfection and frailty, they will see and find in practice quite the contrary. And what was allowed by Father Baker, concerning shifting to get time and means for our prayer, was but in case that superiors did account it but an unprofitable exercise,[4] which

---

2   Luke 23:2; the marginal note here points the reader to Luke 20:23.

3   Presumably, Dame Gertrude refers to Dom Francis Hull's accusation against Dom Augustine Baker, impugning the latter's spiritual instruction as unorthodox or even heretical.

4   The shifting of time refers to the alteration in the monastic *horarium* of the Cambrai community, by which the times for 'mental prayer' (silent contemplative prayer or recollection at set intervals) were changed for her and others who followed Dom Augustine's instruction. Originally, these periods of communal silence fell once after Matins (at midnight) and once after Compline

was the only thing I have often heard him affirm in which he would ever allow a soul to deal in any shifting manner with their superiors under what pretence soever.

And this in itself was never held to be a sin, but an imper-fection, which he also thought it to be. But his reason for his, as it were, winking at their imperfection was to make souls that were apt for prayer to make the higher esteem thereof, and perceive the necessity of prosecuting it daily and diligently too, if they ever desired to arrive to any perfect degree in the love of God. Which esteem, if it had not by such means been brought into the house, it would have been hard for him to have made a soul believe and acknowledge the necessity and nobility of it. For it may be practised by some a long time before they find any extraordinary benefit by it, and till they find the effect of it in their own souls they may be apt to neglect and make no esteem of it in these days when almost everyone of esteem inveigh against it as the most dangerous or unprofitable exercise in the world.

For some hold one of these opinions, and some hold the other. To wit, some hold it only unprofitable; others say it is very profitable if one could avoid the perils of it, which yet in women they hold a thing almost impossible. Which [latter] opinion of the two I most feared, because those that hold it pretend by their objection to have some experience in a spiritual life. And therefore, their words are the apter to make in a soul the greater impression, but, as for the former, it plainly sheweth a mere ignorance in the affirmers.

To be carried away therefore with this opinion and error of the dangerousness of a spiritual life is that which by these writings I intended and desired to avoid by the help and grace of Almighty God. And therefore, when I was clear and not obscured with fear (which I am very subject to) I set down

---

(before retiring). They shifted to falling once after Prime (in the morning) and once in the half-hour before supper (see Augustine Baker, *The Life and Death of Dame Gertrude More*, 45).

these things to be a help and comfort to me amidst the oppositions to that which I have found and experienced so proper and good for me. Which yet, whether it be or no, my superiors will be better able to judge, seeing not only what I believe in all, and my opinion in these things they so much fear our error in, but also my practice in a particular manner.

Now, as for the shifting about our prayer, which is the chief ground of the foresaid public instrument before mentioned that wholly tendeth (supposing our belief and practice to be according) to the disgrace of those who are in that course of prayer and to affright those who come after from following their advice in anything, they being there painted out in plain terms to be enemies to the government of superiors (as having had their instructions by a strange and indirect way and means): I say for all that hath been said in this kind of following our prayer (come on it what will through opposition of superiors), I dare affirm that opinion of Father Baker's [that] hath to us been recalled by him long before the publishing of the instrument. For it was only for an entrance, not for a continuance, since a soul well settled in prayer would not need it, though at first for four or five years a soul by being hindered from two serious recollections in a day by her superiors would have perhaps been in great danger of inconveniency to her progress, and also never have been able to have obeyed as she should. Which is a certain effect of a truly prosecuted course of prayer, supposing it be one who is fit for it. For otherwise it may be very convenient for her to be put into some other course more proper for her. And if she resist superiors in it, she will be in danger of great inconvenience, if not errors, by her misunderstanding and misapplying that which was not for her turn. And this we have in this very house seen and known, which if by untimely hindering (a soul apt for it) a superior procure,[5] he will also incur an inconveniency, though not so

---

[5]   'to contrive or devise with care (an action or proceeding); to try to bring about,

great as hers, which is that she, who would (by prosecuting discreetly a course of mental prayer) have become subject if it were necessary even to a very dog, becometh for want of that strength and help, which therein she got, to be almost impossible to be ruled by the wisest man in the world.

For living in Religion (as I can speak by experience), if one be not in a right course between God and our soul, one's nature grows much worse than ever it would have been if they had lived in the world. For pride and selflove, which are rooted in our soul by sin, findeth means to strengthen themselves exceedingly in one in Religion, if she be not in a course that may teach her and procure her true humility. For by the corrections and contradictions which cannot be avoided by any living in a Religious community, I found my heart grown (as I may say) as hard as a stone, and nothing could have been able to have mollified it, but by being put into a course of prayer by which a soul tendeth towards God and learneth of him the true lesson of humbling herself. [Finding] which effect [...] by following Father Baker's plain, simple, easy, and sweet instructions, I was loath to change them for them I could not understand.[6] And, for this reason, by all the means I could imagine I have endeavoured to strengthen myself by writing, gathering, and thus (as in some part of my papers it will appear) addressing my speech to our Lord.[7] This way is so plain and easy that as long as the soul holdeth humility it is impossible for her to err to her great inconveniency,[8] at least in her main point, which is the love of God. For it less

---

esp. to bring (usually something harmful) upon a person (obsolete)'. See oed. com, s.v. 'procure', v. I.1.a.

[6] That is, she was not willing to exchange the instructions of Dom Augustine Baker for other instructions, which she could not understand, as will be explained below.

[7] Among other short prayers and meditations addressed directly to God, she also presumably and primarily here means her *Amor ordinem nescit* or *Confessiones*.

[8] 'harm, injury, mischief; misfortune, trouble'. See oed.com s.v. 'inconvenience', n. 3.a.

imports[9] for smaller sins – her imperfections and errors or bangors[10] (speaking of such as are accounted such by some precise and exact persons), [such] as to overshoot herself in that in which another would have come off with honour or some such point no way greatly to the purpose as to any hindrance to her course. Yea, by these things (I say) she rather gaineth than loseth, since many times they are a great occasion of humility to her soul, which much advanceth her and is above all chiefly necessary for her. For love [of] God and true humility increase the one the other and are inseparable companions.

In fine, as to the point of following prayer, when the superior [at] that time would otherwise employ her (which I was speaking of before), I say that after the soul hath been some good space practised in that exercise, the superiors cannot hinder her in it by imposing that which to them seemeth fit. And the soul will have no desire to resist them, neither can she do it without a check from God Almighty. For no employments which religious women have in Religion can hinder them (after they have had a good entrance) that the superiors can impose upon them. For, if they pray not at one time, they can easily pray at another or, best of all, pray with the work itself and make the work their prayer.

This therefore being so, that Father Baker did this at first but as a shift in the beginning. There is no just cause to find such fault with it, he doing it for these two reasons: first, because some chief superiors had so poor an opinion of prayer that they thought they did God good service when they hindered them who seem to make esteem of it; the other reason, because those he gave his instructions to and seemed to him most fit for them were likely to come into place of authority and thereby were not only themselves to suffer much by the continual oppositions they were like to find, but also were

---

9   'to be of importance or consequence to; to matter to; to concern, have to do with'. See oed.com, s.v. 'import', v. II.6.
10   An old slang word for a lie or error. See oed.com, s.v. 'banger' n[1] 1, first example.

to bear a great part of the others' burdens which were more fearful and had been a lesser time practised in the course, who yet were likely (if they were encouraged) to prosper very well in a spiritual and internal life. These two were, I say, in part his reasons, which made him go so far in this point. And yet we that had these instructions delivered by him had them with such circumstances that we could not possibly take liberty in anything that was contrary to our superiors' minds by his books or words.

And verily, I may with a safe conscience affirm that, if I would never so fain, I could not find anything in his books nor in any of his instructions on which I could ground myself (without a check in my conscience for doing the instructions wrongs) to neglect, omit, shift off, or sleightly to perform anything of my superiors' commanding or ordaining. Nor could I ever infer anything out of them but that they tend only and wholly to humble the soul, and urge her to seek, desire, and rest in God alone. And this I dare affirm under all the oaths in the world, if justice by lawful authority should exact the same of me. For not any book which he hath writ hath ever tended to anything else than that we should live with all submission and subjection to God and our superiors. And if he had taught the contrary, an extraordinary effect of it would have appeared in us before now, we having been dealt with (being ourselves in authority) as we have been. And indeed, in such manner that no human instructions could have enabled us quietly to have supported the same. The grace of God only, and tending to him by the way of love, could do it, which so humbleth the soul that no difficulty or disgrace can happen which she expecteth not, and therefore [the soul] is abled willingly to embrace the same.

Verily, I can affirm this by my own experience: that a cross word or a slight reprehension, before I was in this course, was more insupportable to me and did more disquiet my mind than all the difficulties and disgraces which have fallen upon me since have done. For now, methinks, though I be neglected by the whole world, by flying to our Lord he easeth me of all my burthen. And as I have desired to have no friend or comfort but him, so it pleaseth him, neither in doubts, fears, pains, disgraces, nor any other miseries (whereunto this life of ours is so subject) to reject me. Only he exacts of me that in all the contradictions he sends me I humble myself and be confident of his help, which, if I do so, I shall be much more sure than if in mine own hands I had a most absolute power to help myself.

And this humble confidence maketh one's way so clear that the soul hath few or no questions in many years, though they have such very near that are never so well able to resolve them. This want of questions is almost all the ground of difficulty between these souls and the confessor, who thinks himself neglected to have souls have no more business with him than in mere confession. But I know not how the souls can help it, though thereby they should offend the whole world. It seemeth to some a great presumption that the soul seemeth to think herself fit to guide herself, and also by it they infer that she sleighteth others (though her superiors) as not fit to govern her, so ignorant do they think she doth esteem them. But God and her own conscience knoweth that none of these things are the cause of her being so reserved, as indeed she is, unless she be asked by them. Which, if she be, they will see that she doth not in any kind sleight or neglect them, yet in speaking she useth discretion where and to whom (for one superior may be fit to be treated with in one point and another in another), which none can judge or term a breach of obedience. And yet this is the furthest that ever Father Baker taught.

And who would not think it a mere folly, if I out of pretence of obedience and greater perfection should treat with one in matter of conscience (in which I were doubtful) who had such difficulty with me in his nature that he were as little able to judge in my case as I were in mine own? For my part, our Congregation giving leave for it and wanting those who are able to judge aright in my case as well as in others, I should do not only myself an injury thus foolishly to go to work but also him whom I should thus treat with upon these terms. Which foolish proceeding is not a proper effect of true obedience but rather a fancy and mere folly.

O how far is it then from Father Baker's meaning to teach or allow of anything which may savour of disobedience! It is true that that which those term obedience, who draw it to nothing but a mere politic course (that leaveth by the practice of it in a soul a poor effect in comparison of that which by the vow of obedience God and the Church intendeth) serveth where it is practised to keep better order than where there is no obedience at all (which God knows in these days is too ordinary). For opposing against superiors is a course which cannot stand without great inconveniences. For if God require that seculars should obey the prince and the laws of the realm (so far as it is may be done without offence to his own laws), and if it be required of them that they pay taxes which are by the king unjustly exacted, what shall Religious persons allege for their defence, if after the vow of obedience they resist and withstand their lawful superiors in what they may justly exact (as we ought to judge all to be that is not apparent sin and offence to God)? And better it is to obey in never so imper-fect a manner than to contend and withstand superiors under what pretence soever. For though it be true that some great saints have afflicted their subjects and misunderstood their proceedings, yet we shall always read that the good subject never sought for other remedy than patience, expecting (for their clearing in the matter) God Almighty's good will and pleasure, who permitteth this often to happen without the fault of the subject, much less of the superior who may do that in justice which we subjects are not able to comprehend the cause of. Neither need we trouble ourselves with thinking of that, but regard God in all and walk solicitously with him. And then will all turn to our good, and God will infallibly teach us true obedience, which is a virtue that maketh our life in some sort to resemble the life of the saints in heaven. For they in all regard God and are totally subject to him. They grieve not to see others in higher degree than they, but see it is just it should be in all things as it is; they praise God in all the sins they see committed in the world and are resigned, though they hate sin, and wonder to see such a Goodness as God is so forgotten by men and so little sought after by aspiring through love towards him. This they see, and yet they remain in peace. And so shall we (though in a far inferior manner) if we perform obedience as we ought, and obey God as readily as the shadow followeth the body, by which course we shall become truly happy. And this is our end of coming to Religion, and if we do comply with our obligation in this kind we shall live quietly and die confidently. For the humility that is in this practice will carry us through all things. This way of true obedience and subjection to God in all things is a way which, though we walk, as it were, upon thorns by reason of the contradictions, temptations, pains, and afflictions with which those are tried that must be his true friends, yet the regard that the soul in all hath of him and the love which by all increaseth in her, maketh it seem to her that she walketh upon roses in comparison of the difficulties she suffered when she sought her own will by following it and seeking her own ease and honour.

This is that obedience which Father Baker so much commends and wishes souls to make right use of in their obedience to superiors, which is so immediate a disposition to it and so great a help to strengthen and perfect it and which, if we neglect, in vain do we pretend to practise that towards God. For their ordinances and orders are a most certain argument of his will. And nothing will he bid a soul do contrary to them.

And if it should seem otherwise to the soul, yet by his own words she would know that she were to stand to their judgment till he altered their minds, which he always doth if it be according to his will and necessary for his honour that the superiors condescend. This I am confident he doth teach and hold. And never other doctrine did I ever hear him affirm, and what might be construed in a contrary sense was but to condescend to the imperfection of beginners, who if they had been held to such precise obedience as some would exact of them, they would have been in great danger never to have obeyed rightly at all. For, by exacting virtue and the practice thereof above the grace and ability of a simple beginner, they make obedience and other virtues seem to be by practice an intolerable burthen. And they, by this means, also faint in their way even in their first beginning. Whereas if they had been [taught] to do things with discretion, they would have been able to go faster on every day than other. And this one point is of such moment that for want of true practice thereof, it cometh many times that the burthens of Religion seem so heavy to good and well-meaning souls.

And in this point do most men differ from Father Baker in their direction of souls more than in any other point. And if this course had not by him been held with me in an extraordinary manner and that he had not daily for a long time encouraged me not to be daunted with my sins and imperfections — assuring me that it would all turn to my good, if by prayer I would endeavour to tend to God and use the best means I could (yet with all possible patience with myself for my defects) to reform myself in all inordinate affection to created things and this more by quietness than extraordinary force — I know not what would have become of me. By this means (I say), diverse imperfections to which I was subject (and which I desired [to] yet could not at first reform), fell off by little and little, when God Almighty did (as I may say) see his time. Which was a quite contrary course to that which was extolled by all that ever I met with before, who can give for the most part no other advice than to overcome all things by force and violence.

But God did shew to me plainly in reading Father Baker's books that my way was to overcome myself as I could, not as I would, but expect God's good pleasure in it. And then when he pleased, if I did my best, I should by his grace get the better of that which with all my industry I was not able to overcome. Which made me see clearly my own frailty, and how little we are able to do of ourselves – yea, indeed, even nothing that is good.[11] For when I have been able to overcome myself in a thing many a time, yet, when I have thought myself thereby secure that I was able to do it again, I have failed more than ever before, which maketh me never dare to presume of my own strength in anything how little soever it seem. For if I do, I am sure to fail.

Another thing besides this point of obedience (by a cer-tain person's means) is much feared in us by our fathers, and that is that we sleight, neglect, and condemn all books and instructions but Father Baker's. Which is, as God knows, quite otherwise. For though (as may be gathered by what I have here collected and noted) I do arm myself by all the means I can imagine against those objections which are made by those of contrary ways that I may hold on my way, which seems to be so proper and fit for my desired estate which I have taken upon myself by my profession, I have no reason to alter for ways I am not able to understand, my conscience being satisfied with this I am in and my superiors never yet condemning the same. Yet, as I say, I am far from sleighting other instructions, but hold they are very good for them for whom they may be proper, which they do not seem for me. Because the more I read or hear of them, the more confused and without coherence they seem to be. For I find nothing but saying and unsaying, as it seems to me, as in one place urging most vehemently the necessity of mental prayer and in twenty other places making it a most impossible thing to give oneself to prayer without more endangering our salvation than before.

And where they treat of obedience they treat of [it], as it seems to me, in such manner that it is almost impossible to find out how or which way one may perform it in any certain

---

[11] See RB 4.42.

or quiet manner. But the more they speak of it, the more impossible thing they seem to make it, and verily I could never put it together to make other sense of it (do what I can) than to draw to this, as they express it: that it is a most servile thing and much like that wherewith servants are subject for fifty shillings a year in the world, and no further effect could come to me by the practice of it (as they seem to mean) as to any true knowledge of God, or myself, than would have come by my being a servant in the world – only forsooth by reason it is performed by us in virtue of our vow of obedience, which makes them acts of greater perfections and consequently of much more merit. But this is a subtle point, fitter to be disputed than necessary to be believed. For I know, and that by experience, that it is possible to comply with our external obediences and perform them so that the superior shall have one in good esteem and be able to discover no great defect in our performance of them, and yet the soul [is] as far from knowing what true obedience is as she was when she came into Religion, performing them all that while but in a natural manner. Of which proceeding nothing can be expected but a natural effect, pride and disobedience increasing daily in the soul, which is an entrance (if God prevent it not) to unspeakable inconvenience. But yet, though I could draw no sure and solid ground for a soul by obedience according to such instructions, yet the defect may be in me as to those ways and not in the instructions. For some have affirmed they find much good by them, of which I am exceeding glad. For so souls may live quietly, obediently, and humbly in the house, it is all one to me by what means, or by whom God Almighty doth it. And there are some in the house that I should advise rather to read such instructions than Father Baker's (if I were worthy to give advice). And this I would do if they were both private men, but much more now these instructions are delivered by the confessor whose place deserveth an extraordinary respect, which to my power shall ever be given him or any other in his place whosever he be. But yet I must needs say that of all in this house I could never see but one who could discourse and distinguish points in and of obedience and draw out of them a settled quiet and satisfactory course, but that when he is gone they be as far to seek as they were before in the understanding of it. For another will express it in another manner, and so under all while they live they must, as it were, begin again.

This therefore was that which made me so affect Father Baker's instructions at first when he delivered them: because I saw they were grounded upon God (not upon him) who could never fail whatsoever became of him. And by this regarding God in all, and doing all out of obedience to him, our soul becometh so humble that it liveth in a manner as subject to all she liveth with, as anyone can be to any superior in the world. She troubleth not her head disputing how, which way, and in what manner she shall obey in this or that, but she simply obeys in all as far as her frailty will permit, and as willingly would she be the most abject and most neglected in the house as ever she was willing to do anything in all her life. For having recourse to God maketh her insensible to those things so far as may stand with flesh and blood. And God doth send and give a soul that seeketh nothing but sincerely to love and please him such occasions to humble herself (which to none can be seen, because the knowledge and cause is wholly within herself) that it is of more force to humble her than her being neglected of all the world would be, though that be also a great help and a great favour of God. For her soul can never be pure and free for the ascending to the praise of God till it be very humble, which the more a soul endeavoureth to be, the more peace doth she enjoy, and the freer access doth she find to God and the [fewer] impediments between him and her soul.

For this true humility and obedience to God, which Father Baker doth so urge a soul to in all his words and books, is an immediate disposition to that which Saint Paul wished to us, which is that *our conversation* may be *in heaven*.[12] And never

12   Phil 3:20.

was there such perceptible friendship, love, and correspond-
ence between any in this world (how great soever their love
might seem) as there is between those souls and our Lord and
his angels and saints in heaven. Which though it be not so
perceivable to sense as the other, which is founded upon that
alone, yet by faith and love the soul doth more plainly and
certainly enjoy it than we can be certain of anything which
with our corporal eyes may be seen. And such a confidence
doth accompany his love that she desireth not to be more
certain of anything. She can wish then that she dependeth
wholly [on] her God alone, whose will is above all most dear
to her and to whom she often cryeth out in her soul with the
glorious Saint Augustine, saying that all that abundance that
is not her very God himself is to her but extreme penury.[13]
And therefore she feareth not any want of temporal means.
For she accounteth it too great a happiness and honour that
by the want of that which is necessary for the sustenance of
nature she should have the occasion the sooner to enjoy him,
her only desire, whom while she liveth here she cannot fully
enjoy (because *none can see God and live*),[14] till which be granted
her all things seem as nothing to her. For [her], longing and
sighing only after him, nothing can comfort or satisfy her soul
while he giveth not himself to her. Yet in this banishment
she remaineth content, because his will is by her even in this
life preferred before her own.

Although those instructions before by me mentioned do
much seem to be like the Jesuits, as I gather by their books,
yet I hold them to be nothing so intelligible as theirs, but
more confused by reason he would bring these and Father
Baker's into one, and make a complete life for a soul out of
both. Which, if he[15] (to wit, the compiler of those instructions

---

13 Saint Augustine, *Confessions*, XIII.8.
14 See Exod 33:20.
15 Presumably, due to context, Dame Gertrude here refers to Dom Francis Hull
    (†1645), vicar of the community from 1629 to 1633.

she much mislikes for contemplative souls) can do for his own understanding and practice, yet I shall think he will find few that will be able to do in it as he doth, but will confound one with another and be able with quiet and satisfaction to practise neither.

For those that cannot use any discourse, to be held to it, it doth them little or no good. And those that can do nothing but by the means of discourse will profit as little by other ways. Now for my own part, I do profess I could never find any good by discourse, neither did I stand in need thereof. For it was an easy matter for any that could have given me instructions for the way of love (which is by the exercise of the will) to persuade me that to love God and seek after him alone was a most happy thing, and that it alone was able to make me truly happy. For I did desire this exceedingly of myself and was very desirous to dispose myself for such a course betwixt my soul and God as might make me most pleasing to him and make me not (as I then was) such a stranger to him. And this I thought was by me to be brought about by a means which I was very defective in. And that was by asking of questions of those who were most likely to tell me what I should do to compass this my desire. Which, [having failed] in [this] (and when I did ask was yet as far from knowing as I was before), I thought to get it by reading. And the more I read the less I did understand, which made me almost quite out of heart. But going to Father Baker almost in a desperate case, he told me my way must be by prayer, for which he gave me some instructions according as he delivereth them in his *Idiot's Devotion*,[16] and referred me for the rest in that point to God. Which, he doing and giving all other instructions for other things suitable, I found presently that course of love which I so much desired. And though I went so simply to

---

[16] Augustine Baker, *Idiot's Devotion* (see Further Reading). ('Idiot' of course in the archaic meaning of 'a simple or ordinary person', not the pejorative meaning the word has today.)

work that I desired to know nothing (for curiosity in reading those things which help to this course is very dangerous,
though in themselves they seem but simple), yet God did
make all things to me so plain that were necessary for me to
know that I wondered to see such an alteration in my soul.
Yea, by my saying the Divine Office (of which merely by my
extraordinary memory I had gotten a little understanding)
he did so enlighten and instruct me that no industry of my
own could have attained such knowledge for this my own
purpose of loving God and humbling myself, as I had even
thus for nothing. For my pains and industry were so little
that it was not so much as to be esteemed. And thus, God of
his mere mercy dealeth still with my soul, for which if I be
not humbly grateful, no punishment is sufficient for me. But
I hope, though I be so frail and weak, yet his grace will in all
assist me, which I beseech you to beg of him for me.

It sufficeth not for the soul that there is in God himself,
whom the soul seeketh after, simplicity or unity. But there
must also be all possible simplicity in the soul herself, for the
making her fit to treat with God and thereupon become united
to him. The more simple or one that the soul is (which is that
the more she is free and rid of all thoughts of creatures which
cause multiplicity), the liker is she to God who is simplicity
itself, and the more apt and worthy to become united to him.
And therefore, all the cunning and industry of a spiritual
master should ever be by all lawful means to rid the soul of all
multiplicity, incumbrances, blocks, and all other things that
are enemies to the foresaid simplicity in soul. And indeed,
every image of a created thing is an impediment to the said
simplicity, and therefore is to be rejected at such time as the
soul is in case to apply itself immediately to God.

He that is a true spiritual master will in such a case take
great heed how he lay anything on the soul, lest it cause the
foresaid impediment. Every soul, of her own nature, is apt
to contract multiplicity and impediments enough. And if she
have withal a master to devise and lay more on her, how can

she be but held back and be indisposed for the said perfect immediate treaty with God? And one only impediment is impediment enough and hinders all.

The spirit of simplicity doth bring and cause much peace in the soul for tending wholly towards that *one thing which is necessary*.[17] It maketh the soul as insensible as it can [be] towards all other things, digesting and passing over with patience unkindness and injuries, whereby her life becometh properly a life of patience. Also, as this simplicity is grounded upon plain and simple instructions, so is it and must it withal be, as well, founded upon simple and plain dealing with God and man – simply intending God and avoiding all double dealing and all undue intention.

A true spiritual life should be one long continued thread lasting from the time of his conversion to the end of his life. Saint Paul reprehendeth those *who are ever learning and never come to the perfection of knowledge*.[18] Such are they who, yielding to temptations, lose their supernatural light and fall into a state of less light, which is more natural than supernatural, and therefore is but darkness in comparison of the other light and always is deceitful and erroneous as to the finding of the right way towards God. Whereas the other said internal light within then proceeded from a superior cause or gift that is more supernatural.

The things absolutely necessary
for those who shall begin and prosper
in a true spiritual course
are these that follow

1. Instructions proper for a contemplative life.
2. Secondly, an aptness to understand and practise the said instructions aright.
3. Thirdly, a great courage to withstand all temptations – come they from within or without – that might draw her into

17   See Luke 10:42.
18   2 Tim 3:7.

multiplicity from simplicity, and especially fear, which soon draweth one into the most pestilent multiplicity – that is, maketh one more blind every day than other – and consequently into more diffidence whereby they are made almost wholly incapable of conversing with God, unless God shew them their errors and they begin again, which is a hard matter to do if a soul [has] once lost her light. Which God I beseech him [to] deliver all capable souls from doing. For it is the greatest ingratitude that can be offered to God, and none but God can tell the miseries, perplexities, and difficulties that attend on such a soul all the days of her life (as Saint Angela doth testify with terrible words).[19]

4. Fourthly, there is necessary in the soul a good and right judgment for the understanding of things aright. For else the soul will erroneously understand all things, though never so plain. The more she knows the farther she is to seek, and the more errors she falleth into. And better it were if such souls could be known (which is almost impossible till they have had some knowledge of a spiritual life, for many times they seem to have a greater aptness than the most capable souls and a greater inclination towards God than others, and yet [they] run into error and are in danger – do what they can that have the care of them – to break their brains or overthrow their bodies) that they never had spiritual instructions further than for the active life.

5. Fifthly, a great capacity of tending towards God by the exercise of the will, which, being prosecuted together with true mortification of themselves, will bring, saith Blosius, to a mystic union and perfection in time convenient.[20]

---

[19] Saint Angela of Foligno (1248–1309) describes the terrible effects of her deprivation of the presence of God in the Memorial section of *The Book of Blessed Angela of Foligno*, ch. 8: *Complete Works*, trans. Paul Lachance (New York: Paulist Press, 1993), pp. 196–202. Dom Augustine Baker recounts this passage in his commonplace book, *Book E*, ed. John Clark (Salzburg: Institut für Anglistik und Amerikanistik, Salzburg University, 2002), pp. 37–43.

[20] Louis Blosius, *A Book of Spiritual Instruction (Institutio spiritualis)*, trans.

Of those that have all these conditions there are yet great difference. For some have more aptness and find [fewer] impediments than others. And some have more light, and others less, as it pleaseth God. Yet those that are most humble and faithful to him, though they seem less clear, are the most pleasing to God, who be blessed by all. Amen.

THE OBSERVING OF THE DIVINE CALL, which indeed should be and is the very life of a spiritual life, is by most spiritual masters nowadays turned into a scorn or scoff. And therefore [it is] no marvel that true spirituality should in these days be so rare and almost unknown. Nay, if a soul give but herself to prayer, she shall have an hundred enemies – one objecting against one point, another against another of her proceedings.

Everyone (according to their spirit and humour) [desireth] to reform her in they-know-not-what themselves, which, if she be moved with, no other effect is like to come of it than happened to the painter who altered his work so long and often that at last it had neither form nor fashion. And all others that had procured this alteration in the picture (which at first was a very good one) called the workman [a] fool for his labour.

The application whereof[21] is very plain and proper to our purpose.

First, there is difference between *unity* and *union*, for as *unity* is but one thing, so *union* is a coupling together at least of two things.

Secondly, *simplicity* is a singleness or being alone, and *simple* is single – that is, a thing alone. And therefore, *simple* or *single* and *one* or *simplicity* and *unity* is but the selfsame thing.

Bertrand A. Wilberforce and ed. a Benedictine of Stanbrook Abbey (Westminster: The Newman Press, 1955), V.1, p. 33.
[21] That is, of the 'Divine Call' mentioned above.

Thirdly, multiplicity is a manifoldness of things, and two or more diverse things do make a multiplicity. But one thing and less than two will not make a multiplicity. God and a creature both thought of together as distinct things are a multiplicity – not because [of] the apprehension of God being apprehended [...] according to faith, but because of the thinking of the creature not as in God (for then it would cause no multiplicity), [as] a thing distinct from God. And a creature alone, thought of without any apprehension withal of God, if it [is] not to be termed multiplicity (which it is in the takings of mystic authors), yet is it not most certainly the simplicity in soul that is required for union with God.

Fourthly, God is but one thing, or a unity, simplicity, or a singleness. For though all things and all diversity of things be indeed in God, yet they are all of them but one thing in him. Yea, whatsoever thing or things be in him they are God himself. God was and is that *one thing* (which our Saviour, defending Saint Mary Magdalen, said to be) *only necessary.*[22]

The imperfect contemplative spirits, who commonly in their external businesses are in their interior full of multiplicity, do yet for all that, when their businesses are laid aside and they betake themselves to their recollection at the season proper for it (in regard they have as it were a natural and habitual propension towards God and his immediate presence with a loathing, or at least a neglect or disesteem, of all creatures as to any affection to them), easily surmount all multiplicity of images that could be occasioned by their precedent employments, wherein their souls had never fixed their love, as [persons] who were not nor could be satisfied or much delighted with them.

All the spiritual men in the world are not able by their instructions to make another, that yet of herself is most apt

---

22 See Luke 10:42. For this traditional identification of Mary of Bethany with Saint Mary Magdalene, see note in 'Of Suffering and Bearing the Cross' above.

for it, to become truly spiritual without[23] the scholar herself do withal carefully observe and pursue the foresaid lights and Calls, as her *primum mobile*, or first mover. And to say 'Take all your instructions from without', is all one in effect as to say, 'Tend not to contemplation'. For God, and none but He, is the true and immediate teacher and director in the most obscure and supernatural way of contemplation. Yet here I would be understood that under these terms of divine interior lights, motions, and Calls – which I take to be the root and cause of all her true obediences and other good needs – I intend and comprehend all calls through other obligations, as when they are otherwise commanded by the universal divine law, natural or positive, by the Church or other human law, or by the wills of superiors. And a true spiritual man should do nothing but out of the said root or cause, which is the Divine Call.

A supernatural discretion is imparted by God to a well-minded soul that disposeth herself for it. Which disposition consisteth chiefly in the use of abstraction[24] and prayer. This is the light by which God guideth souls which he leadeth to contemplation, and thereby teacheth them what is necessary for them to know or do externally or internally, so far as conduceth to the said end. Simple and unlearned souls, by the said light, come to find out those internal ways most obscure of themselves, which no man (though never so learned and acutely witted) can discern or find out of himself.

The most spiritual man in the world cannot instill this light into another. All he can do is exteriorly to teach a soul how to dispose herself for it. And as a soul that hath never so great a capacity for it (speaking ordinarily) cannot find it out without the help of some experienced person, so one that hath no aptness for it, all the teachers in the world cannot put it

---

[23] 'simply as a conjunction: … except, unless'. See oed.com, s.v. 'without', 2.
[24] 'the action of withdrawing or secluding oneself from worldly or sensual things, or of turning one's mind away from the world toward the contemplation of the spiritual; a state of solitude or concentration on the spiritual arising from this action'. See oed.com, s.v. 'abstraction', 1.

into her. And those that have the aptness can never find true comfort and satisfaction but in contemplative instructions, and being once well instructed will find all things preach them to her in their kind. Nor will she understand anything she reads or hears but in that sense if it be to any purpose, finding that to be her only secure way and all things to help her thereunto, if it be not her own fault,[25] how much soever the aforementioned meddlers mislike of her proceedings and misinterpret them. So, one that hath not that aptness will misunderstand all or most of those instructions and wonder how they can be practised without falling into this or that error and taking this or that liberty by them, thus measuring others by their own understanding of things.

This was always thus and ever will be – be the persons never so holy – God permitting it for the exercise of both. I mean only amongst women; for men, though they should be defective in practice, yet they have it by speculation if they be scholars. And verily I am of Saint Teresa's mind that learned men are not so apt to put souls out of their way as the unlearned are. For if the unlearned be spiritual, and not truly spiritual, it is incredible the martyrdom that a contemplative soul hath to undergo being under his charge. And young mir-acle it will be for her (if she has not many to encourage her) to hold the instructions proper for her and in which only she can prosper, and out of which, if he should put her, he would be the first [except] only herself that would be weary of her. But if she hold patience it will fare with her as it did with Saint Mary Magdalene: that our Saviour will answer for her as far as it is convenient for her obtaining *the best part, which shall never be taken from her.*[26]

Nothing is more improper for a contemplative soul than to contend, complain, or justify herself, all her remedy for the most part being to come from silence, patience, humility,

[25]   That is, 'unless by her own fault'.
[26]   Luke 10:42.

and resignation. I except where justice doth require a simple relation of the truth to superiors when the good of her own or other souls in the house requires it. And that she must never do suddenly or out of passion or aversion, but it behooveth her to consult the matter often and seriously with our Lord, and in the meantime to behave herself humbly to the party or parties and do them both with God and man all offices of true charity she can.

The supernatural light, or discretion, is to be nourished and increased by all the external helps that can be afforded. And great heed is to be taken that it be not obscured or destroyed, as God knows it may easily be if we look not well about us. And the least mote of darkness defeats the whole sight, God permitting it for our sins and negligences when it happeneth.

This light is commonly never given but where the internal senses are naturally adapted and made proper for the receiving and using of it. And therefore, extravagant imaginations, though otherwise never so devout or of never so retired natures, are incapable of it, yea, are in manifest peril to mistake at least of making right use of it, misapply, and misunderstand (to their great prejudice and others' great inconvenience and trouble) this doctrine of the Divine Call. And better it were, if it were possible, that such souls should never so much as hear of the Divine Call.

This confirms that old proverb which sayeth, 'one man's meat is another man's poison', and so it is in this. For a soul truly apt for contemplative instructions can never find any solidity or certainty in another thing than this: [...] observing of the Divine Call in all things. And [she] finds that it is at hand at all times and all occasions to be her guide and directrix. Such a capacity is there in our soul to have relation to God in all cases, and in particular it is necessary in doubtful cases. For where he determineth it by obedience or necessity, it were to tempt him to desire him otherwise to declare his will to us. So, as I say that, as the soul can find no comfort or certainty in any other instructions, so on the other side nothing is more perilous to be misunderstood by those that have not an aptness for a contemplative life or the internal exercise thereof, though otherwise never so good souls and of never so good meaning.

None are capable of rightly understanding and practising this instruction of the Divine Call, but they who are resolved to deny themselves in all things and who wittingly and will-ingly adhere to no created thing. For if the [soul] do willingly retain an affection to any thing, she is at a stop and can go no further. For God must be sought and loved wholly, if we desire and endeavour to arrive to perfection.

This observing the Divine Call was that, surely, which Saint Augustine speaketh of in his *Confessions*, where he lamenteth his case of darkness and blindness before he had given himself wholly and seriously to the service of God and to observing and living according to his justice. These are his words: 'And I was not then acquainted with that true interior justice which judgeth not by custom but by the most righteous law of Almighty God'. And certainly, the better disposition the soul is in of living and walking in this light and according to this justice, the better will she prosper in a spiritual life, and the more clear will her way be, and the less peril of erring. For it is the way of humility, and none but the humble can walk in this light long or find any gust[27] therein.

They will either leave the light, or the light will worthily leave them if ever they had it.

Tauler[28] saith that God rewardeth no works but his own. The purer our intention is in doing, suffering, or forbearing, the more is it his own. And the more perfectly a soul com-plieth with her duty toward God (in that manner that he

---

[27] 'keen relish, appreciation, or enjoyment'. See oed.com, s.v. 'gust', n. 2.4.a.

[28] Johannes Tauler, OP (*c.* 1300–61): German mystic and theologian, disciple of Meister Eckhart, OP. See 'Sermon for Epiphany', in *The History and Life of the Reverend Doctor John Tauler of Strasbourg with Twenty-Five of his Sermons*, trans. Susanna Winkworth (New York: Eaton and Mains, 1907), p. 234; Johannes Tauler, *Predigten*, ed. Georg Hofmann (Freiburg: Herder, 1961), p. 32.

exacteth of her and is proper to her state, and the grace given her), the more she pleaseth God. And in this respect it is truly said that *obedience is better than sacrifice.*[29] For we do never so much, if it be not that and in that manner God requireth it of us. We shall live in blindness and find no peace in our soul, for God hath ordained a certain way and means for every soul for her walking and profiting in the way of perfection. And in that only will they find their progress to consist: to observe what it is God exacts of them and enables them to and not what others do or can do or have done. For as we all differ in face, so do we differ in the manner of our exercises that are interior. As, for example, if one who is of a free nature and can endure little abstraction should force herself to as much as those who are of staid and retired natures, and to recollect herself in time of work and other times in which by order of the house she is to keep silence (which exterior silence she is to observe), she would but hurt her health and, it may be, her head, and not well be able to recollect herself then nor at the proper time for recollection, and so lose all for want of discretion. Whereas if she should do what she is able and no more, and abstract herself by little and little, as God shall increase his grace, she will in time be enabled to that which will be sufficient for her. And God will require no more but what he hath given, which how little soever it be, we ought to account it more than we deserve. And employing that well, he will increase it, who is more willing and desirous to give than we can be to receive. If we live so retiredly as he will enable us, we shall easily perceive what he doth require and exact of us in everything. For we, being Religious, are by obedience and necessity for the most part disposed of. And for the rest we have God always present to consult with. And when we cannot by that means be resolved, he will shew us how and where we shall otherwise be resolved. But those that go the way of true humility and mortification will have few

29   See 1 Sam 15:22.

questions after they are well grounded and instructed in a spiritual life. For, for the most part, our questions do but tend to the winding ourselves out of some cross or mortification or easing our mind of some difficulty, which will if we yield thereto but put out our eyes, and consequently put us out of our right way – yea, though those we consult with be never so spiritual or understand our case never so well. And of these I have been most afraid of all, for from others we can easily restrain ourselves, but from them, upon pretence that we may ease our minds and at least do ourselves no harm if it do us no good, we often cause great prejudice and obscurity to our souls. And yet when all comes to all we must suffer [what] we do, if we will be the faithful servants of God and profit in a spiritual life. If ever God do stand to his promise (as ever he did and will to all his promises) [of] granting when he is asked or opening to those that knock,[30] where or when will he fulfill such promises more truly and certainly than in the case where a simple and sincere-meaning soul out of necessity and with all resignation and humility begs at his hands the solution of that that concerns her for his service and honour, and the salvation and perfection of herself in his love?

The more a soul holds herself to this light and walks by it, the more her light increaseth. And the more she leaves this light and walks by another seeming-light, the more her darkness increaseth. The clearer this light is in her soul, the better able she is to judge what is the just and most righteous will of Almighty God in those things which faith and obedi- ence hath not determined. For what one is bound to believe and do for salvation, the Catholic Church doth determine. But what we are to do for perfection, there may be many different opinions. Yet all agree in this: that it must be the way of abnegation. But for the rightly applying of spiritual and contemplative instructions to one's own particular, he is the only able teacher who is the most true love and light, the

[30]   See Matt 7:7.

Holy Ghost, of whom the author of *The Scale of Perfection* writeth to his scholar, being a woman, thus: 'For grace' (which Father Baker termeth a 'call') 'shall even teach thee by itself, if thou wilt but observe it and follow it till thou come to the end, all that is necessary for thee from time to time. For God alone can teach this way'.[31]

And of those who give themselves seriously to walk in the way of perfection, Saint John speaketh thus: *But you have the unction from the holy one and know all things, and the unction which you have received from him, let it abide in you, and you have no need that any man teach you, but as this unction teacheth you of all things, and it is true, and it is no lie. And as it hath taught you, abide in him.*[32]

There are two reasons or necessities why God himself should take on him and perform the office of a contemplative master.

1. The first is because he can and none but he can. For, though the soul may have an instruction from another, yet is she to make use of it but according to her internal master's direction, and as if he, and none other, had given it to her.

2. The second reason of convenience or necessity of God's being the teacher is that, though man also could resolve her doubts and give all directions both internal and external, yet were it not only inconvenient but even impeditive to her in her way to contemplation by reason of the solicitudes[33] and distractions the soul would incur by such occasions as causing a life merely of distractions. For in some souls there do occur to be resolved frequent and daily or hourly passages[34] in the forepart of a spiritual course (especially in the interior), which

---

[31] Walter Hilton (†1396): English Augustinian canon and mystic. See *The Scale of Perfection* (Kalamazoo, MI: Medieval Institute Publications, 2000), II.42.

[32] 1 John 2:20, 27.

[33] 'the state of being solicitous or uneasy in mind; disquietude, anxiety; care, concern'. See oed.com, s.v. 'solicitude', 1.

[34] 'an occurrence, incident, or event; an episode in a person's life'. See oed.com, s.v. 'passage', n. IV.14.

of themselves are questionable. But such going forth for reso-
lution would mar all in a contemplative spirit, as causing a life
merely of distraction and multiplicity, and those the most profound and pernicious distractions, as being upon mere[35] internal matters. For solicitudes about the interior are the most
prejudicial that are as to tendance to contemplation, because
they most obscure the soul, and yet this is the miserable life
of scrupulous persons. Whereas the soul having always her
master at hand – and that nearer to her than she is to herself,
and he an infallible one and a most quick dispatcher – all the
mischiefs of the precedent case are avoided and she satisfied
in her questions with all sufficience and security. Neither
will it be sufficient for the soul in these excursions that it
is judged a reasonable occasion to ask a question by him she
consulteth. For if it were a thing wherein God himself would
have resolved her, if she would have had patience or else that it
were a thing that for her mortification he would have had her
ignorant in, she will perhaps incur much obscurity for such
going forth without her internal master's leave and liking, and
withal such a check in her conscience that she could with more
case have endured the displeasure of all the world than have
thus displeased her beloved, whom alone she desireth, intendeth, and thirsteth after and to whom to adhere and inhere
she putteth all her content and happiness. All he doth and
permitteth seemeth most just and reasonable to her. And to
live interiorly and exteriorly according to the right rule of his
justice is all she desireth. These are they which (our Saviour
said) should *Adore him in spirit and truth*,[36] and of whom it is
said, *All the glory of the soul is within, for the kingdom of God
is within us*.[37] Such a soul may truly say, *I will hear what my
Lord God saith within me*.[38] This my most sweet Lord God be

---

35 'without admixture or qualification; purely; exclusively'. See oed.com, s.v.
    'merely', adv.2 1.a.
36 John 4:24.
37 See Luke 17:21.
38 Ps 85:8.

ever adored and praised and sought after by us all and blessed and praised by all in heaven and earth forever and ever. Amen.

Tauler saith that it is as easy for one that hath an aptness for an internal life and [that] will be diligent and observant in it to note, observe, and discern the Divine Call within him, as it is for one to discern his right hand from his left.[39] And it is plainly our Rule that our holy Father's desire is that souls should observe their internal Calls and the tracts of the divine Spirit who is that proper master of the interior.[40] And it is but a mere natural course that we can run by the mere instruction of man, from whom only we have our first help and instruction, and then the souls capable of living a true internal life are to be referred to God, the only Teacher of the way of Spirit.

And where it is objected by those who pretend to be spiritual that following the divine tracts, motions and Calls is perilous dangerous and without warrant or security, it may be answered (supposing always an aptness in the party that hath the instructions) that as the power of God surpasseth the power of man, so the warrant and security of God, which a true internal liver findeth from God, is far beyond the warrant of a mortal man, the warrant of one man being contradicted by another. That from God is able to stand in all the contrarieties, changes, and oppositions which happen out of the differing of all men in indifferent things. For, as for other things, God refereth the soul to the ordinary means he useth in those cases. As, for example, for confession of mortal sins, she must confess them to a priest who hath jurisdiction over her, and for a true doubt she must not presume that he must resolve her by himself, but she must ask according to discretion and obedience. And for

---

[39] I have not found this statement in Tauler, though a similar emphasis on one's discernment regarding what is best in the spiritual life can be found in Sermon 29 in Johannes Tauler, *Sermons*, trans. Maria Shrady (New York: Paulist Press, 1985), p. 106; Johannes Tauler, *Predigten*, ed. Georg Hofmann (Freiburg: Herder, 1961), p. 203.

[40] See for example RB 20.3–5.

her Rule and other obligations of Religion, she must observe them out of obedience to God and superiors. Which being done, and also going and walking the way of the cross, what warrant, I pray you, will she need (after her conscience is once well settled) from confessor or superior? Woe be to those, at least woe in this respect, that have a confidence rather in men than in God, and those that praise so much the security of a soul that hath no other confidence in God at her death but so far as she is warranted by her confessor, for she cannot but by this means die perplexed and troubled. For today I have a confessor which will warrant me and tomorrow another who will doubt of my case. Today I have one so precise that he will warrant me in nothing, and tomorrow I have one who thinketh he can pierce so far into all things that, if I will adhere unto him and nobody else, he will answer for all. He goes away, and another who must assist me at my death cometh, who is of a good meaning but cannot pierce so far as the other; he at first finding us to fear, feareth too; we have forgot our courage upon the other's warrant going before and fall into fear with him at the present. And yet our soul doth not alter before God according to everyone's apprehension we meet with. If it did, or if this were all the certainty that were to be found between God and our souls in Religion, we might bid all true confidence *adieu* (I mean those only who are apt for an internal life, for as for others I do not take upon me to know their case) and place our peace upon that which is as changeable as the moon – to wit, the humours and opinions of men in indif-ferent things. I have had myself a confessor who, though he had the largest conscience that ever I knew [a] good man [to] have in my life in what he pleased, yet out of the difficulty he had with me in his nature and out of his aptness thereby to take all I did and said in another sense than I meant it, he could and did turn twenty things (which my other confessors made no great matter of) into horrible mortal sins and would have frighted me from the sacraments till I had settled my conscience according to his will and mind. What was I to do in this case? I had been warranted by three former confessors, two of which were my chief superiors and doctors of divinity, and now this present wholly doubted my case. He had (as he pretended) a greater reach into my case than all the rest, and they were simple to him in discovering truly the state of my soul. But should I in this case put my soul into his hands, who desired to know all that had passed in my life to inform him in some things he desired to know out of policy, thereby also to tie me to himself more absolutely? Verily, if I had thus put myself on him, I had done great wrong to God. And I might have bid farewell to all true peace hereafter. But standing to my former warrant and giving him the respect was due to him, and being reserved towards him, I have hitherto (God be praised!) kept myself out of his fingers. And also, by the grace of God, [I] hope to hold on my way in tendance towards God, thereby raising myself (according as his divine majesty shall vouchsafe to enable me) out of my natural fear to the love of God, who is only able to satisfy and satiate our soul. And not, as this my confessor would have had me, to plunge myself by reason of his words and threats of[41] my miserable state, which, notwithstanding his apprehensions, is so much and no more as it is in the sight of God, who changeth not his opinion of us as the humour of the confessor may be but imagineth us according to what we really are in very truth. But these spiritual men of this kind would be so absolute that there is no power left in the soul thus under such to have relation or confidence in God, whereby those for the most part under them, if they be poor simple women of how good spirits soever, live miserable dejected lives. For it is their only way to bring their politic[42] and absolute government about. And ordinarily under this pretence they do it: saying that there is no way to make this or that soul humble but to bring them into such fear that they neither dare speak,

41 That is, 'concerning'.
42 'policy; politics'. See oed.com, s.v. 'politic', 3.

think, or do anything without their approbation. At least so far they must have relation to them as it may serve this turn: to inform them of what is for their purposes. And then that soul is happy in their eyes, and they will declare that they are so to others, that they might follow their example. Then the perplexity the soul suffereth they term a profitable pill to cure their disease withal. And the confusion they suffer to see themselves disloyal to God and man to serve their confessor's turn, he termeth a suffering for justice and warrenteth them what harm, disquiet, or confusion soever cometh by this their doings to others or themselves out of obedience to him, he will answer for it. And therein they have done God and their Congregation great and faithful service.

O misery, that all this should be fathered upon holy obe-dience, the most noble of all virtues! Who sees not that this is a turning of Religious obedience (in those that simply desire to perform it) to a policy abominable to be thought or named? O my God, was this thy meaning when we vowed ourselves to thee? Or rather, didst not thou say, '*Be as wise as serpents and simple as doves?*'[43] Thou didst not say, 'Be so foolish under pretence of blind obedience that thou shalt not know thy right hand from the left'. Thou bidst us *give to Cae-sar what is Caesar's and to* thee *what is* thine.[44] By truly obey-ing thy will, law, and evangelical counsels, we grow wiser. But by pretending to practise obedience, charity, humility, patience, etc., in perfection before we be ripe for it (through perseverant prayer and concurrence of thy grace which doth not such things suddenly) we lose all and live in blindness, and the highest we come to is servile fear and mere folly. O happy are they to whom God giveth an aptness for an inter- nal contemplative life and withal someone who may instruct them in it. Verily the most part of souls in this house, who have been fit for it, have been satisfied with so few instruc-

---

43   Matt 10:16.
44   See Mark 12:17.

tions that in a manner they might be expressed in five lines.[45] As, for example, that they transcend fear and tend to God by the exercise of the will, by which in time (as pleaseth God) all impediments shall be removed between God and their souls. Which Blosius warranteth a persevering soul in his *Institutions* very confidently.[46]

But, alas, those that are not in this simple way have such an apprehension of a spiritual internal life and make it seem so perilous and dangerous that souls would be frighted exceedingly to read their books and hear their sermons (which cannot be avoided possibly) if they were not armed with armour of proof by God and those who live in and walk this happy way of simplicity. Which whosoever truly walketh will not condemn, much less contemn,[47] those who speak against it, but humble themselves in all things, knowing that others who live extroverted lives may be more pleasing to God than they and that for many reasons which they may easily conceive. And yet it doth not hinder these, at least it ought not, from prosecuting their ways to which they are called and in which by God Almighty's infinite mercy they have so many books of Father Baker's own writing and transcribing to encourage and comfort them in all the opposition which God doth permit only for our exercise and not by it that we should be put out of our way through our defect in patience, which the very exercisers of us would for the most part be very sorry for if it should so happen, howsoever the public instrument and other speeches do sound to us. For who can doubt (that is a wise man) that a soul that hath a good and sound natural

---

[45] In the printed book, the following explanation (leading up to 'Which Blosius...') takes up five lines of print. One wonders if this reflects a similar wording in Dame Gertrude's original manuscript that specified however many lines the same content took up there. In the absence of an original manuscript, this is left at guess work.

[46] See Blosius, *Book of Spiritual Instruction*, III.8–9, p. 29.

[47] 'to regard or treat (a person or thing) with contempt; to reject (a person or thing considered unworthy or undesirable); to scorn, disdain'. See oed.com, s.v. 'contemn', 1.

judgment, solid contemplative instructions, many in the house that practise the same doctrine aright, and a quiet nature, seconded with concurrence of God Almighty's grace, and goeth in all the way of abnegation and resignation, should pass many years without cause of questions about her interior? For who doubteth but the soul may love God more and more every day and extend her will as infinitely towards God as she can and bear all occurring difficulties with as much patience as she can and perform her ordinary obediences by the orders of the house and particular ordinances of superiors with as much relation to God and out of obedience to him as she can – and all this without any great questions? Yea, the foresaid course of spirit, in a manner, taketh away all occasion of questions (at least, of intricate questions) which draweth the soul out of her interior more than into it. And by the way I say this: that those souls who are apt to ask questions, though they be never so quiet, devout, innocent natures or have never so much wit and judgment, they will never prosper in a contemplative course and in those instructions. And therefore [they] will do well, and much better, to take the ordinary instructions of these days. And it were well if such souls never heard nor read contemplative books and instructions, because [their] misunderstanding them will make both themselves and others also with them to lay the defect which was only in them upon the unfitness of the instructions for woman. For it will seem to them that they cannot possibly be practised by women without perils and dangers unspeakable, which wrong done to souls put out of their way by this means (who would have happily prospered therein) redoundeth to the dishonour of Almighty God. But yet, as it seems to them that they cannot be practised without great danger, so those on the contrary who are fit and capable for these ways see and experience how little peril there is in them. For can a soul be too humble, and love God too well? No, certainly. And this is all the course of this internal life, and to this only it tends: to love God and to humble ourselves.

Let us therefore make that benefit God willeth we should by these oppositions and contradictions we find and feel from our order – to wit, to humble ourselves in all and behave ourselves with all respect and obedience to them, as if they had done nothing. Let us encourage one another to this, and let us not think God cannot be well served by any other course than this. For certainly the Jesuits, who have the perfection in their institute of the active life, are in a very proper course for their kind of life. For that spiritual exercise which they yearly take doth them much good and maketh them deal with the more pure intention in their actions and affairs, being also strengthened with a daily recollection which maketh them foresee many inconveniences, and thereby prevent them better than they who do give themselves to no such thing. For who can think but it helpeth a man much to proceed with the more prudence, when by a certain retiredness he hath so much foresight of his businesses and occasions? They have also a settled form or fashion in all their proceedings and exercises, which those whom they take into their order must conform themselves to, how apt or unapt soever they be for it in their nature. And they, having indeed the choice in a manner, of all the prime wits of their schools, are easily able to find those who are able to uphold and maintain that politic manner among them. The main point of upholding and maintaining of it being the exact obedience which they require of all, and which, all with one uniform consent standing upon and performing, they thus, as they do, uphold the same form and grow in all too hard[48] for all other orders, they being all in a

---

[48]   That is, 'rigid'. Dame Gertrude's point here seems to be that the Jesuits' disciplinary programme is so strict that it is deemed unsustainable by those outside of the order, and yet the Jesuits themselves, because of their ability to select their membership, will continue to uphold that strictness despite what critics outside the order will say. The fact that Dame Gertrude's spiritual director before Dom Augustine Baker seems to have persuaded her and the other nuns to adopt spiritual programmes based on Jesuit models seems likely to be at play here, though she does not come right out and say so. This contributes to her larger point about due consideration for the proper fitness (or 'aptness')

manner divided amongst themselves, and these of all nations standing against all the world for themselves. Besides, the subordination is also much strengthened with the fear they have, who desire to make any resistance (how little soever), of being put out of their order, to their perpetual infamy and shame and want withal of that which is necessary, which they are incident to who leave this order.

This, I say, helpeth them to the power of disposing, without any resistance, of any under them, according as it may be most for the temporalities and honour to the order. Withal they have a great regard to the employing of men according to their abilities, having almost all the best employments at their disposing. (And that is a great matter to the maintaining of their order in greatness, for, if they wanted abundance of action, their order would quickly fall into great desolation.) And this is the reason, as I conceive, which maketh the nuns of contemplative orders prosper so ill under their hands: because they put them into exercises of discourse and yet withal do not go about to bring their houses into subordination which they have amongst themselves. And besides, they cannot find these poor women sufficient action to employ themselves in. And therefore, out of the abundance of wit which they get by that superficial recollection, they devise and make for themselves unnecessary and unprofitable action. And this was in the light of truth certainly foreseen by their founder, Saint Ignatius, when he absolutely forbade them the care and government of Religious women.[49] And with this his foresight I wish he had so provided that they indeed had never meddled or undertaken in this kind. For better it is for women to be kept in their ignorance whereby they would be

of a given spiritual course for each soul, which she expands upon below.

49   The relevant legislation is found in Saint Ignatius of Loyola, *The Constitutions of the Society of Jesus and their Complementary Norms* (Saint Louis: The Institute of Jesuit Sources, 1996), Constitutions VI.588; Ignatius of Loyola, *Constitutiones Societatis Iesu et Normae Complementariae* (Rome: Curia of the Superior General of the Society of Jesus, 1995), *Constiutiones* VI.588.

the more easily ruled than to be puffed up with knowledge so little for the good (and so far short of what is necessary for the perfection) of their souls. Yet hospital nuns make a good shift[50] with their instructions, which sheweth plainly that those who follow their kind of sensible exercises without going further or looking after a more spiritual prayer of the will must be held in much action, or else they will be apt to make a great stir. But in enclosed monasteries, action sufficient in this kind is impossible to be had or found. And therefore, I wish with all my heart that either this course were not amongst such so much as known or else that they rested not in these first exercises but proceeded to the most noble – yea, as Seraphinus Firmanus[51] saith, to the omnipotent exercise of the will. Which, if it were now practised in our and other contemplative orders as it should, quickly would they surpass in knowledge and all moral and divine virtues those whose furthest pretence in these sensible exercises is but to do their actions with the more deliberation and consequently with the more humane discretion, which it gaineth indeed. But it is, but in a manner, a mere natural proceeding. Only so far as it may be grounded in faith and charity it deserveth both more praise and reward than a mere natural action. But how far those proceedings are from leading a soul to perfect charity, which is the end of our coming to Religion, may be seen by the few saints which it now produceth. And though they have a great advantage by their uniformity in exercises and their agreement among themselves, yet this being generally accounted to proceed and to be upheld by policy, it worketh

50 'available means of effecting an end'. See oed.com, s.v. 'shift', III.3.b.
51 Seraphinus Firmanus (1496–1540): Canon Regular of the Lateran, author of several Italian works on the spiritual life translated into Latin. Dom Augustine Baker cited Seraphinus Firmanus in his writings. I have not been able to locate Firmanus's use of 'omnipotens' to describe the exercise of the will, but three particular discussions of the will suggest its prominent place in the contemplative life in the printed publication of Firmanus's works; see *Ferventissimi Verbi Dei praeconis* (Vincentium Comitem, 1570): pp. 230, 255, 564–6.

no great effect for the most part, further than by it with all others and against all others to serve their own turn,[52] which is a quite contrary effect to that which that order produced when it was in its prime by having in it some great contemplatives, and when they did so much good and were so beneficial to the whole world. And different also from that which our order and others were, when in like manner they flourished with saints. For then the honour of God was sought, and all orders with one uniform consent did concur to the advancement of that alone. They then applied themselves to several exercises in the exterior, everyone according to his institute — some more easy, some more strict; some of more action, and some of less. Yet interiorly their end was all one, that was to find God in their souls. And out of that, perfect charity did grow in them by those internal exercises. They did everyone (not out of custom or because he was of such or such an order), as God did require and enable them, employ part of their time in gaining and doing good unto souls. Then there was not such solicitous entangling and, as I may so say, sole care of temporalities, God taking care of them and casting them on them. Then there was indeed perfect amity without interest or fond[53] affection to their impediment of loving and seeking God alone, who is that *one thing which is only neces-*

---

[52] The earlier editor of Dame Gertrude's writings, Dom Benedict Weld-Blundell, inserts a note at this point in the 'Apology' to acknowledge the rather severe tone our author has adopted. He points out that, given the problems that the Benedictine convent at Brussels had with Jesuit direction before the founding of Our Lady of Comfort and the problems Dame Gertrude and other nuns of Our Lady of Comfort had in the early years of their founding (when it seems Jesuit models were encouraged), Dame Gertrude's tone toward the Jesuits can perhaps be excused. Dom Benedict points also to her youth as a reason for the severe tone here, and suggests that 'no doubt, if she had lived longer, she would have found occasion to modify her views' (pp. 253–4, n. 1). While I take Dom Benedict's note as being generous, I also think, with a hundred years of history between our perspective and his, we may be less likely to deem Dame Gertrude's attitudes toward her male superiors unduly impertinent without more information.

[53] 'infatuated, foolish, silly'. See oed.com, s.v. 'fond', A.2.

sary.[54] Then there was no exceptions of persons, but they were contented so [long as] God's honour were advanced by any as well as by their own order or themselves. O Lord my God, if this spirit might be revived again, how much would my soul rejoice! If Saint Benedict's, Saint Augustine's, Saint Francis's, and Saint Ignatius's children were all (as perfectly as this life would permit) united together and did with one heart and consent seek and labour to advance thy honour and praise, as our Founders do wish in heaven, then would the spirit of the primitive Church flourish, and thy torn and mangled members of thy Church be healed and perfectly set together again. Then sinners and heretics would easily be converted by them to thee. Then there would be another learning than now there doth flourish in our order and others'. For thou by them wouldst speak, *who makest the tongues of infants eloquent.*[55] Then they, by prayer conversing in a familiar and tender manner with thee, would speak so that none would be able to resist thee in them.[56] Then their judgment would be so cleared that they would understand most hidden mysteries. Then an hour of prayer would instruct them more fully than an hundred years study can do if they have not in all things relation to thee, the only true wisdom and *in whose light is true light* only to be seen.[57] By loving thee and dying to themselves in all things they would become masters of themselves and all the world. Then nothing would move them, nothing would affright them, because thou wouldst be their comfort and stay in all things. Certainly, there is a wonderful difference between the obedience which a soul that liveth an internal life giveth to a superior and that which we give out of custom. The former is slow at first and seemeth very defective therein. The other so violent many times at first that it con-

---

54 See Luke 10:42.
55 Ps 8:2.
56 See Luke 21:15.
57 See Ps 36:9.

tinueth not long. The former groweth more strong and firm every day than other, and the latter groweth oftentimes a greater burthen every day than other. Certainly, a soul that pretendeth to live an internal spiritual life and yet hath not a great esteem of obedience is much to be feared and in great peril of errors. Yet that which in these days is termed obedience I do not mean. For I knew one[58] who, having a confessor that had much difficulty with her though he affirmed that it was a great breach of obedience to have relation (while he bore that place) to any other, yet she made use in cases of difficulty (with leave of an higher superior) of another, whom she thought more able to judge in that which concerned her. And yet, she hopeth this was no breach of obedience, for if she had thought that God in this case had exacted of her not to have gone to another, she would (what difficulty soever she had endured) have made use of no other. But this she thought was not his pleasure, because she was in a probability to fall into great inconveniences if she treated with him in an inward manner who professed by his deeds and words to take advantage of anything [he] could that might serve his turn as far as he could in conscience. Besides, the difficulty he had with her in his nature made him incapable of judging aright in that which belonged to her, for that difficulty of his made him misapprehend all she did or said. If she held her peace she neglected him; if she spoke she did it to sound him to serve her own turn; if she was compassionate towards him in his infirmities, she flattered him; if she offered him not that which he stood need of, she was averted from him. And thus it passed between them, which made her have as little to do with him as obedience to higher powers would permit her. For by their order she was to confess weekly to him, which was no small difficulty to her. But she, knowing it to be God's

<hr />

[58]   Given what we know of Dame Gertrude's relationship with Doms Francis Hull and Augustine Baker, it seems entirely possible that she here means herself.

will, did it out of obedience to him to whom if we do as we ought we must be subject in all things without exceptions.

And this is the benefit of an internal life that makes one capable of seeing and knowing God's will, and also most ready to perform it which way soever he signifies it to them, and makes them obey as readily and willingly a simple, impertinent superior as they would an angel or the wisest creature in the world. Yea, if a worm or any creature were ordained by God to rule over them, they would see and embrace with all their hearts his will by them, for without this total subjection to God it is impossible to become truly spiritual. For if we resist his will in our superiors, in vain do we pretend to please him. We must learn therefore this virtue of him, that true humility and obedience may be our stay in all, which two virtues together with the divine virtue of discretion he will teach us, if we labour to become more and more humble. For, seeing that it is his will we should obey and become truly humble, how can we doubt but he will give us the grace, if we humbly and perseverantly beg it of him and practise them upon occasion as well as we can? For he himself saith, *When we ask our father bread he doth not give us a stone, nor if we ask him a fish he doth not give us a serpent.*[59] Much less will he deny us what is necessary to make us pleasing to him, if we seek or desire nothing but by true love to be faithful to him.

O prayer, prayer – able to obtain all things! O how cometh it to pass, my Lord, that this omnipotent prayer, as some of thy dear servants style it, should be so unknown? Yea, even by them, whom thou termest *the salt of the earth,*[60] contemned – at least as to the practice of poor, simple women, for whom they hold it above all things most dangerous even to mine own knowledge, as I have known affirmed by superiors of several orders! O misery to be lamented most heartily by those that have a taste in prayer and by the effect thereof know how

[59] Matt 7:9–10.
[60] See Matt 5:13.

sweet a thing it is to attend only and wholly to the praise and love of God! Surely, the want of the wisdom which by prayer the saints did gain is the reason why custom in all things doth take place (for the most part in the world) of true reason. The world surely was never reformed of sins and errors but by the wisdom which cometh from God and is far different from that which is accounted wisdom by the world, which is, as Saint Paul saith, *foolishness with God*.[61] For the wisdom of God proceedeth out of humility and perfect charity. This wisdom did Saint Francis enjoy, when yet by the world he was desirous to be accounted a fool, which opinion though many had of him, yet the effect of his wisdom was evidently seen by the great reformation he made in the world.

It will never go well and peaceably in the world as long as they are only employed and have the spiritual government of souls who take policy for their chief ground next to faith, which, in the order and manner of their writings in these days, methinks they seem in all to pretend. For they prize that most which may serve their turn and suppress all orders but their own (though not in plain terms) as far inferior to them in all things. And that indeed it is not so to me seems evident, for I know none but may be compared to them in all things but policy. This is my simple opinion: if the soul hath not so much wit or discretion when she knoweth for certainty or else doubteth of the certainty of a thing that concerns her; or, knowing that certainty, will go and ask it as a doubt; or, taking it as a doubt, seeing need to ask, will not put herself to ask – I may warrant her from ever coming to contemplation. *Whosoever are led by the Spirit of God, they are the children of God*.[62] As Saint Paul said, if we were the perfect children of God, his Spirit would live and reign in us. But for as much as yet we are not, we are seriously to labour to be, and *that he*

61 1 Cor 3:19.
62 Rom 8:14.

71

may be all in all with us and in us[63] and his divine voice and will only regarded and executed, and none but his. And let us take the greatest heed that can be of lessening the worthy estimation of the Divine Call that in itself is the prime verity or divine way proceeding from it. Let us extol and commend it as we would do God himself and dispose us and all others as much as we are able, that in all things it may be observed and fulfilled by us all.

But O Religion: no Religion where the knowledge of the Divine Call is, as it were, unknown, unless it be in speculation or perhaps, through ignorance, is persecuted, depraved, obscured, derided, banished, and sought to be pulled up by the roots and kept out of the hearts of those that desire it or are capable of it! Surely, God will take all this as done to himself and revenge it in an extraordinary manner, except where invincible ignorance excuseth this proceeding. But yet for the verity of this doctrine, or the general practice of it, God will never permit *the gates of hell to prevail* so far as to be able to extinguish it,[64] because it is the root and cause of all sanctity in his Church, howsoever he may permit it to be lost out of the hearts of some particular persons through their frailties and the working of others. And surely, *nisi quia Dominus erat in nobis*[65] — *unless that God had been in us* — and holpen of late more than man did or could, *obscuratus penitus fuisset pusillus noster sol, et versa in densissimas tenebras tenuis nostra lux* — *our little sun had been wholly obscured, and our small light turned into a thick darkness* — by the late proceedings, by writings, preachings, speakings, threatenings, libellings, and other actings of some persons, the Divine Call had been exploded, clean lost, and abandoned.[66]

---

[63] 1 Cor 15:28.

[64] See Matt 16:18.

[65] Ps 123:2.

[66] The editor of Dame Gertrude's book, Fr Francis Gascoigne, notes at this point in the text that: 'The Religious father whom she chiefly points at for opposing the free following of the Divine Call and Father Baker's doctrine did, upon

But God would not suffer it, neither will he. Yet far be it from any man to say or think that it was directly intended or maliciously done. It was at the most but indirectly at *sine omni prava voluntate*,[67] and without any intention. But God only and their own consciences know what hath passed therein by the occasion of the said late proceedings. I mean what fears, what doubts, what perils, what shakings, what internal probations, explorations, purifications etc. *Sed benedictus es Domine Deus meus, qui adiuuisti nos, et consolatus es nos, qui ex magna tentatione magnum fecisti prouentum, qui ex tenebris lucem creas, et veritatem ex erroribus et falsitate facis magis clarescere. Mane nobiscum in aeternum. Instrue, conforta, stabili, veritas tua maneat in aeternum, Spiritus tuus bonus nos instruat, dirigat, protegat, et ducat in via quae ducit ad te. De nobis caeci sumus, et lux non est in nobis. Viue, regna, et splendesce intra nos, dissipetur et in nihilum redigatur nubes tenebrarum et ignorantiae. O vere et sole sol! Adoramus te orientem, fruamur lucente, quia deficimus deficientes. In te et per te spiremus, respiremus, et expiremus.*[68]

his deathbed, repent him of it and was very sorry he had done it, professing himself never to have been any true practitioner of such spirituality and that he had taken upon him that which he could not judge of. And he further declared that he much liked and approved all entirely what Father Baker had written and taught'. The priest referred to is Dom Francis Hull (†1645), vicar of the community from 1629 to 1633.

67 'without any malicious intent'

68 'But blessed are you, Lord my God, who have helped us and have been our consolation, who have brought us success in great temptation, who create light from darkness and make truth to shine out clearly in place of errors and falsehood. Stay with us unto eternity. Instruct and comfort us, make us firm, and let your truth remain with us unto eternity, your good Spirit instruct us, direct us, protect us, and lead us in the way that leads to you. We are blind of ourselves, and there is no light within us. Live, reign, and shine forth within us, scatter and render as nothing the clouds of darkness and ignorance. O true and only Sun! We adore you as you rise, we enjoy you as you shine, for we who are insufficient ceaselessly fail. In you and through you may we breathe life, take breath in, and expel it'. The three verbs in this last sentence are of course pregnant with overlap and resonance in Latin (spirit, breath, life, drawing in and blowing out of breath, death) that pale in English translation.

Superiors, in my poor judgment, after they have granted and declared most ample and almost all possible authority to their deputies (for the government of poor fearful souls that might have been ruled according to God's will with less than a beck[69]), have need to have an eye and good respect to matters, and not expect that God must always do for their safeguard that which themselves might do.

They speak with little consideration who say [that] it is enough to do what a counsellor adviseth, especially in virtue of his place or office. Unless they regard withal that the soul hath been so taught by God or man that she knows how to use such counsel for her profit, and namely for contemplation. For if this were so there would not be such scarcity of illuminated persons as there are. And I have known some who have been so obedient that they never did anything contrary to their superior's will, nor refused to do anything that was enjoined them by their superiors—yea, further, were so inward with their superiors that they seemed one heart and one soul with them. And yet for all that they affirmed in my hearing that they were as ignorant of God and as great strangers to him as they were when they first took the habit—yea, not altogether so fervourous and devout as when they entered into Religion seven years before. So that it seems either the superior must be spiritual to make his subject so, or the subject must be so spiritual as to know how to benefit himself by his obedience and other exercises, or else he will never come to perfection, let him have never so great aptness to a spiritual life, or read or hear never so much to that effect. For where we read of great supplies on God's part for and in works of obedience, either the subject or superior was an illuminated person and had a great regard to God in that which was done or com-manded—that it was his will and what he would have to be done in it he did clearly see in his interior. For if some dispo-

[69] 'a mute signal or significant gesture, especially one indicating assent or notifying a command'. See oed.com, s.v. 'beck' n² I.'

sition were not required in the party or parties for God to do and supply great matters in the soul by that bare word – 'do it for obedience' – a superior might by the command have God so at his command and at a beck that he commanding his subject to come to perfection or to do such or such a work in such and such perfection, God should presently enable the soul to do it so – though neither the subject or superior knew what perfection were further than by speculation. But the expecting of such miracles is absurd, for God hath ordained another way to come to perfection. And never any by this course come to find out the right way or ever attain to that degree of perfection which is so much spoken of, and even out of ignorance exacted and expected the first day of taking the habit – to wit, of blind obedience. Which yet, in some sort, some who have good and quiet natures attain to (but the clean contrary way to that which they should do) – to wit, to a blind obedience without sense or reason, never going further in it or by it than to a natural perfection. Which, though it be much extolled by those that see her and is better for her soul than to obey only in what she list and no more, which is another extreme, yet she grows but by this into favour with superiors and into credit with those with whom she lives, and into a certain natural perfection of mortification which little benefitteth her soul, and for which, if she look not well about her, she will receive her reward in this life – to wit, by satisfying and contenting herself with the good liking and applause of her superiors and companions and thinking that if she can please them she dischargeth her duty to God as to her obligation of tending to perfection. But if there were to be no other effect of all our mortifications and abstractions and other obediences in Religion, I should say, woe is me that I was Religious. But to this may be answered that by our vows and virtue of our profession we have a double merit for all that we do. Whereas if we were not Religious we should have but a single reward, and this the Church by her power and the superabundance of the merits of our Saviour (of which she hath the distribution by way of indulgence or by virtue of vows made by souls that are in the favour and grace of God and, consequently, her dear children) imparteth to us that are Religious. But to this I reply that if this were sufficient the world would never have been fuller of saints than now, for there were never more Religious. And yet none will deny that the world was ever so without saints as it is at this day since Christ's time. Which plainly sheweth that there is to be some other disposition in the soul for her advancing by the exercises of Religion and that the having made the profession and living laudably therein in the sight of others is not sufficient for her before God, nor the pretended examples of former times, nor that blind obedience which is so much extolled and commended by all to be exacted in perfection of her before she have found good entrance into her interior by prayer and abstraction and can regard God in that which is to be performed by her and, by the good disposition that is in her soul, turn it to good and not to the obscuring of her soul. For otherwise it will be blind obedience indeed and obscure her soul so that she can neither perform that nor anything else as God doth require she should. Which, if she do not, it will little avail her that others like it.

By which you see that only living in Religion and pleasing our superiors will not advance us in the way of perfection, nor practising a blind obedience which hath in it neither reason nor discretion. And presuming to practise virtues in perfection before we are come to any perfection is to break our necks for ever coming to perfection. Can a soul of a year's standing in Religion take upon her to become to Abraham's perfection? Surely, if she do, I should hardly expect to see God prosper that her presumption with an Abraham's reward. It is plain therefore that we may very absurdly oftentimes apply the examples of saints to our poor, imperfect case and get little by it. Yet this is not to disapprove of a soul's prompt obedience, for that is most laudable. And those souls who are in a contemplative course and endeavour nothing but by entering into their interior to be able to regard God and his will or Call in everything they do or omit will grow more obedient and submissive every day than other and perform that which is said, that they should be subject to every living creature for God. Which those other hasty and inconsiderate persons who will practise everything presently in its perfection will never arrive to, but, rather, for their hastiness (if their natures be not the better) they will be found more stubborn, rebellious, and more hard to be ruled fifteen or twenty years after their coming into Religion than they were the first day. And then they will look for these and [those] privileges: their antiquity forsooth must be respected; they must be exempted from prostrations; and if they have behaved themselves more submissively and obediently than others (though it were but merely out of the quietness of their natures), they must be observed, respected, and preferred in Office before all others, or else they have infinite wrong. And they pretend if they be neglected it will be a cause of others' less obedience and respect to superiors, who, they say, will rather prefer others that will not take it well to be thus humbled than one who may be made a fool of, as I have been all this while, and it seems ever shall be. Had not superiors better wink at a little want of too much forwardness in an imperfect soul who doth it merely out of consideration of her own frailty and that she may not obscure or put out that little light which by much labour, care, and industry she hath through God's grace and assistance gotten in her soul for the finding out and walking in the way of perfection and contemplation? Yes, certainly. It were far better for superiors to pass over some slight imperfections, which have no sin in them, in a soul who seriously laboureth for perfection. For such a soul will give, as it is given her. That is to say that [...] God, of his mercy and goodness by her conversing with him, by her suffering that he lays upon her with the best resignation she can, and by observing the Divine Call and will and living according to the justice of God, shall strengthen her soul and purify it in his love. And so much the more prompt and ready to obey will she be and give every day more and more respect to superiors.

And there is one thing in this virtue of obedience prin-cipally to be observed and practised to make it pleasing to God and an advancement to the soul. And that is that the thing commanded and done be according to the justice of God. But to this may or will be answered that all that is not a sin, if it be commanded us by our superiors, is according to the justice of God. But if this were so, so many more would come to perfection than do. And it would be far more easy to come to it than it is. But perfection and sanctity must be gotten by other means than by persuading ourselves that we shall come to it by simply doing, from time to time, what our superiors willeth or biddeth us. If, withal, we do not in our interior regard God in his justice as well as the exterior bidding of superiors, and do it more out of regard of that than the other—yea, as much as is possible (if we will do it well)—we are to do it with a simple pure regard of God and his Call. For though the interior Call never contradicteth the exterior (for if it do, it is to be shrewdly suspected) and that, for the most part of things to be done in Religion, God calleth the soul by exterior obedience, yet it is his will that in all those things as well as in mere internal [things] the soul should simply regard him, and that as absolutely as if he by himself had bidden or commanded her. Neither doth such a soul regard who or what or in what manner God requireth it at her hands, but it sufficeth her that it is he that exacteth it of her, whom she in simplicity of spirit endevoureth to regard in all things without any means of creatures. Which maketh the soul indifferent whether she were commanded by an angel or a worm, if it were God's will rather to command her and signify his will to her by the worm. Not that she esteemed not of the angel in a far higher degree, but because she would not make anything her object or do anything out of other respect than to conform herself to the divine justice in all things and regard him alone in all she did or omitted.

And certainly, let a soul be persuaded or persuade herself what she will as a means to perfection, she shall never find true peace (if she be of a contemplative spirit and be not defective in her natural judgment) but by following the Divine Call and regarding that in all she doth or omitteth and, though she do all that superiors command, yet to do it with as little regard of them as much of God as if he had immediately commanded her by himself.[70] And so much as God shall by his grace (concurring with her care and diligence) enable her to work in this observation of the Divine Call, so much the more light she shall have for the observing of it, so much the more profit and peace will she find in her own soul, and so much the more shall she walk according to the justice of God, of which, how much the more our works do partake, so much are they worth and no more. For, as Tauler saith, 'God rewardeth no works but his own'.[71]

Where it is said in our constitutions that after our profession we have not so much as power over our own bodies or souls, I understand it that by the very nature of our profession we are so bound to tend to perfection that we should do nothing but in regard to God, whose will we have here professed to choose for our own. And whose justice we will with all diligence perform, let him signify it by what, whom, and in what manner he please without any regard of our own profit or commodity for time or eternity. And certainly, in this sense obedience cannot be too much commended. But let our actions be never so much commended and applauded by our superiors and all others. If it go not right between God and our souls, it will be but little to our comfort or profit. And if we reflect upon the circumstances of the superior's command, whereby we may obscure that regarding God in

---

[70] RB 5.4.
[71] Johannes Tauler, 'Sermon for Epiphany', in *The History and Life of the Reverend Doctor John Tauler of Strasbourg with Twenty-Five of his Sermons*, trans. Susanna Winkworth (New York: Eaton and Mains, 1907), p. 234; Johannes Tauler, *Predigten*, ed. Georg Hofmann (Freiburg: Herder, 1961), p. 32.

our souls, we shall never become perfect in obedience. For as Saint Paul saith, *Power was not given for destruction but for edification,*[72] and applying it, performing it, and exacting it in another manner than as it was meant and ordained by God in and by our Religious profession is the reason that so few become perfectly obedient. For by making our obedience to regard superiors in the first place – for example, to trouble and perplex ourselves in thinking it must be done with this circumstance and this manner and at this time, and diverse other circumstances little to the purpose, or else I shall not perform my obedience in perfection – this is to tire out myself and make myself weary of obedience, and not to serve God with alacrity, and cheerful willingness. This is to find his *yoke* intolerable and not *sweet and easy,*[73] which certainly, if it be not to us, it is our own fault and not his. For he hath set such order and measure in all things that the more they are done according to his will the more easily are they done.[74] For he is far from being the author of disquiet and confusion; his Spirit *is justice and peace and joy in the Holy Ghost.*[75] And it is we that by our preposterousness do pervert his justice and cause that effect in our souls by that which we pretend he exacts. And so (as Sir Thomas More saith),[76] 'the urchin wench goes whining up and down, as if nothing she did or could do (for some circumstance or other which was wanting in it) did please him', who yet indeed is so easily pleased by those of good wills and who intend or desire nothing but to please and content him and seek him simply and purely, not any gift or grace, but according to his will, [so] that if there were no world but this and that my soul were to die with my

[72] 2 Cor 10:8.
[73] See Matt 11:30.
[74] See Wis 11:20.
[75] Rom 14:17.
[76] Here a marginal note says, 'This Sir Thomas More, the famous Lord Chancellor of England, blessed and renowned martyr of Christ Jesus, was her great-great-grandfather'.

body, yet I would choose to serve and please him alone, and none but him, rather than by doing the contrary have all others my friends and have all the honours, pleasures, and, in fine, the whole world at my command. And this, though I were also to suffer and subject myself for his sake to every living creature whilst I lived. For in this kind of life lieth hid the greatest heaven that can be enjoyed upon earth. And though he try the souls with diverse temptations, yet he doth it with much regard of their frailty and doth so accommodate his grace to that he layeth upon them that they find he reserves that for tomorrow which the soul was not able to have borne with profit today. And the soul so plainly sees that she of herself is able to do nothing, so that if she had overcome one difficulty or temptation a thousand times, she dareth no more confide in her being able to overcome it again than if she had never done it yet in all her life. And yet, she is so confident in God that if it were pronounced unto her by God himself (who cannot deceive or be deceived) that there were infinite disgraces, pains, temptations, poverties, and confusions hung over her head, all the care she would take would be to beseech God continually that, as he provided those troubles for her, so he may enable her to bear them without offending him therein and in that manner for his glory that he intended by sending them. For of herself she willingly acknowledgeth that no feather is more easily carried away with a violent wind than her soul would be carried to hell by the least temptation the devil could suggest unto her if he did not in all things by his grace protect her. And the longer and the more faithfully a soul hath served our Lord the clearer doth it appear to her that, whatsoever is well done by her, it is so wholly to be attributed to God [and] that she deserves most just punishment if she take any part of it to herself, or presume by what she hath done by his power to be able to endure the least cross that can befall her of her own self.

But to return to that I was speaking of – I mean obedience – I say (in the words of a most learned man, Albertus

81

Magnus, master to the divine Saint Thomas of Aquino) that, so far as any virtue partakes of discretion, so much of virtue hath it in it and no more.[77] So that, if a soul practise humil-ity, charity, obedience, and, in fine, any other virtue without discretion, it will more partake of folly than true virtue, as the effect in the practiser will show. This discretion is the pure gift of God. The which he never so abundantly bestows upon any but that they are all their life to have relation daily and hourly to him by prayer, in which he teacheth them as far as it is necessary for them what they are to do or what means they must take to know what is best to be done in all that they doubt of. For, whether he resolve them by himself or by others, they acknowledge it to come from him, neither do they desire to be their own choosers in this or anything else, and so it comes all to one pass as to them. For they regard him alike in all things. Neither can one, generally speaking, apply another's case to oneself without danger, because the circumstances may much differ and so make that in them a folly, which was in another perfection. Which many times we blindly do, and no wonder if we prosper accordingly. For in all things we are to have relation to God and do what he exacts, and not what is the custom or what this or that body hath done in the like case. And if we do otherwise, we shall be as blind as beetles and never prosper in a true internal, contemplative, spiritual life. And for want of well practising this point many get no entrance into their interior all their life, though they have in them a very great aptness for it. And this point I have before touched in one place of these my notes for mine own remembrance, which I have written down either as I heard them from Father Baker or as they came into my

---

[77] Saint Albert the Great (†1280): German Dominican friar and bishop of Regensburg, early scholastic philosopher. See Albert the Great, *Paradisus animae, sive Libellus de virtutibus* in *Opera omnia*, vol. 37, ed. Augustine Borgnet (Paris: Ludovicum Vives, 1898), pp. 498–500, esp. p. 499; *The paradise of the soul. Or a treatise of vertues* (Saint-Omer: English College Press, 1617), pp. 221–30, esp. pp. 223–6.

head when I was least obscured with the passion of fear to be a help to me or at least some little light when I was not so well able to help myself.

And reason I had, having so many occasions to try me within and without and put me into perplexity and fear. For one in eminent place did labour by his objections to divert me, though not with ill intention, but out of a pretence of putting me into a course more proper for me. As, for example: because I was full of imperfections, he pretended that contemplative instructions were no way proper for me and that I took too much liberty by them, they being proper for those of more tender and fearful consciences than I was. And, in fine, gave it me under his hand very resolutely as a determination from my ghostly father, as in the place of God Almighty, that those that gave me contemplative instructions and applied the liberty that was necessary for contemplative souls (of which he saith there are not two in all the house) to me, might give me peace but never true peace in God. These were his words which did so much astonish me that it made me purvey[78] for all the instructions that I could that might uphold me in that which I found was the only way that I could prosper in or be able to find our Saviour's *yoke sweet and his burden light*.[79] For I had suffered so much before God did bestow the favour upon me of being put into a course that was proper for me, and this for near five years after my coming over, and had fallen into so many great inconveniences and miseries that none could believe it but I that felt it. And though I made a shift adays to set a good face on it, yet in the night I bewailed my miseries with more than ordinary tears, of which God and our blessed Lady were witnesses of, though few others on earth. And I did rouse up all the books in the house, and whatsoever I found that any had done to please God I took notes of it and did it as I could. And this course I always held since I

[78]   'to foresee; to see before; to consider'. See oed.com, s.v. 'purvey' III.8.
[79]   See Matt 11:30.

came into Religion: as also to consult with all the men that any had found good by in the house. And yet, all this would do me no good. And methought I was as great a stranger to Almighty God as I was in England when I scarce thought (as to any good I did) whether there were a God or no. And being thus perplexed and tossed with a thousand imaginations and overwhelmed with miseries – yea, almost desperate through the fear and consideration of my sins – my mistress advised me to go to Father Baker, telling me that four or five in the house had found good by him and that at least it was no harm to try, and it would do me no harm though it did me no good. For he was a very grave man and one that was much respected in the Congregation. Suchlike words as these she used to me, and I in my nature being not very hard to be ruled (though I remember I had not great mind to it of myself) did as she bid me, which being done I found myself in fifteen days so quiet that I wondered at myself. The which was so soon as I had received from him some general instructions, as that I must give all to God, without any reservation wittingly and willingly of any inordinate affection to any creature. The which I found myself willing to do. And that I must use prayer twice a day, which I found myself capable of. And though I found little of that which is called sensible devotion, yet I found that with a little industry I was able to use it with much profit and that it did make anything very tolerable which happened to me. Yea, and it made me capable of understanding anything that was necessary for me in a spiritual life and discovereth daily to me that which is an impediment between God and my soul, as far as is necessary, and makes me abhor to do anything in the world for any other intention than out of the regard of God and because God would have me so do. And I find by and in the exercise of prayer, God doth find such means to humble me that all the creatures in the world could never have found them out for me, and also sends me such internal crosses and shews me yet so plainly what I shall do in them (if I will advance my soul by them as he desireth) that it were but to obscure my soul to ask questions about them, and, will or nill I, I must bear them. And thus, I see that God doth so temper everything he layeth upon me, that it is so much and no more than I am able to bear and is convenient for me. And methinks I see that anything I overcome is so wholly to be attributed to God that I cannot presume to be able to endure the least cross in the world and should think it an extreme presumption to expose myself to hazard by willfully putting myself of mine own accord to the suffering of anything but what obedience and necessity provideth me, which I find to be enough.

Thus, upon occasion I have foolishly strayed from my pur- pose and now I return to the matter of applying blindly the practice of saints to our imperfect case. For God will prosper us by those exercises that he thinketh good and not by those of our own inventions. If the soul simply regard God in the best manner she can, it will be as easy for her to see what he would have her to do or omit (I mean in things that are not sin) – when to ask, when to hold her peace, when to pray and how to pray, etc. – as it is easy to discern her right hand from the left or the sun from the moon. But this will be if she go the way of abnegation and not else, and if she rest in God above all creatures and have relation to him as well as she can according to her imperfect state in all things whatsoever, either in general or particular manner, as the case requireth. For we cannot prosper any other way in a spiritual course or by any other means than the divine conduct. And this not prospering any other way or by any other means than God pleaseth may be very well applied in some sort to the case where the director out of his own head and out of his own customs would have the soul pray in that manner he hath good by. And if God lead her by another way than he hath gone, she is wrong, howsoever it be indeed. And if the soul be full of perceptible imperfections in her outward carriage, and if in occasions she be apt to overshoot herself sometimes in jest, sometimes in earnest, then he will determine she is not fit for internal exercises unless they be very gross and sensible ones. And if she will not believe him in this so far as presently to relinquish her former directions, she goes astray. Into which directions, notwithstanding, she hath been put by the advice of her chief superior and found, by prosecuting what she had begun, that her soul was reformed by little and little and that she was willing and enabled by God's grace to amend any particular defects that the confessor found in her and reprehended her for. Only when he misliked her course and would not tell her why nor wherefore but in a confused manner, she stood upon her guard and held her peace, having before endeavoured by all information she could [obtain] and as well as she could to express herself, that she might do things with his good leave and liking. I say she held her peace and was confident that her course was never the worse for his fearing and meant not by the grace of God to alter it, till superiors by diligent examination of her (which she most willingly will accept and give them all the information she can as she hath done him) should judge thereof, to whose determination she finally meant to stand. For my part, I say I shall follow her example the best I can. But if besides her imperfections he by some inward discourse perceived by her (when she was in some darkness and much obscured for that time with the passion of fear) that she had some scruples of her former life which troubled her, though indeed she had been advised by two who knew her conscience as well as she could make them and who were men of as much respect as any in her Congregation, and one of them her chief superior and the other her director for many years, notwithstanding, I say, she had both their warrants for what she did under their hands and, indeed, finds herself checked in conscience by God himself in an extraordinary manner when she doth in this point yield to follow her own sense, desire, and fear rather than what they have advised her. Yet I say, if this ghostly father of hers should think it not only fit but altogether necessary to bring her into all fear he could, pretending that the liveliness of her nature and the great courage she had could not be abated with anything else than with letting her and advising her to dive into her conscience and case as much as she would, and that she could never come to profit but by laying a good foundation by this means, which he pretended was so necessary for some things which he discovered in her that it was hard (if possible) for her to be saved unless she did proceed in this manner, what would you advise the poor soul to do? I will tell you what I do, and upon what reasons I do it, as well was I can.

1. First, for the ill ground which he said I laid,[80] he grounded it upon these reasons: first was upon the unsettledness he thought was in my conscience, which indeed was as it is at sometimes in which humour he once lighted upon me. And as to this, I comforted myself that I needed not to fear, seeing I had done what I had been advised to by the said two upon whom I relied in it. Nay, also when he was better able to judge my case, he advised me the very same himself. As also when I am in prayer and most clear, I see I cannot please God by any other means than by standing to the advice that hath been given me by the said two in this kind.

2. Secondly, he grounded himself upon a conceit that I held so constantly to the course I had been up into before he came out of policy, because I would not be taxed with inconstancy and also because I might lose the interest in those who had the same instructions and that partly because they were many of them, the most eminent persons in the house for natural talents. But to this I answered myself that, as for policy, I did not well understand it. And so far as I did understand it, I did abhor it even out of this respect: that those who practised it (in the nature I understood him he meant) lead miserable lives

---

80 Dame Gertrude here switches from the third person she uses to relate this person's case immediately above to the first person in her response. One assumes that some inconsistencies in presentation remain since it does not appear she prepared this text for publishing.

and must oblige themselves more to the humours of many to bring their ends about (than the love of liberty would have permitted me if I had had no better intention), and yet for the most part miss of their ends in that which they most desired and perhaps undergo great disgraces in having their plots discovered. This, I say, if I had had no other intention would have made me abhor it. But I also comforted myself with this: that since I first entered into this course, I never desired the friendship or favour of any creature living, not so much as durst wish deliberately that anything should happen otherwise than it did. And when I thought it for the honour of God and good of the convent, I did not fear any disgrace or difficulty that could happen unto me in that I thought fit to be done. And what I did in it out of other intention or natural inclination, I desired that God should purge me for it by any contrary success in the business as he pleased.

3. A third reason he had (as the aforementioned writing of his gives me to think, as I understood it) was out of this respect: that I was cheerful, merry, and free, notwithstanding he had judged my case to be so bad and perilous, whereby he might think that I sleighted his admonishment and was insensible of my own miserable case. As to [this], I had these reasons to comfort and help me. One was that reflecting upon my own conscience between God and my soul, I saw no cause but that it might hope that matters went well between him and me and that I was never the worse for his fear of me, and some things he charged me with I found myself innocent of, and some others I found myself guilty of I endeavoured the best I could to amend. Also, for my shewing myself cheerful, it was partly to bear up myself and partly because I thought that was the way to make him the sooner to let me alone, as indeed it happened. And another reason was because I am naturally sad and had more than ordinary exercise at that time, which made me more subject to it. And also, I find it necessary to be as cheerful as I can, because nothing obscures my soul and hindereth my prayer and transcendence so much as yielding to sadness.

I also perceived both by his writings, words, and sermons that he in all things almost misunderstood my case, that though he were very spiritual as for his own particular and in a course that he seemeth to me to prosper very well in and which was apt to be much applauded by the admirers of sensible things, yet he was far short of being able to direct a soul to contemplation who was in nature and by grace apt for those instructions that tend to it. And I perceived also that although he could savour almost no books but those of con-templative authors, yet he still misunderstood them so in his application of their writings to others that all his proceedings turned rather to the breeding of dangerous multiplicity in the soul than to the riddance, which is so absolutely necessary that without[81] the director help the soul in that, in vain is all he can do to her, as to her coming to contemplation.

I also perceived that he misliked the happy instructions we had received (and which caused in me so much peace and com-fort after so much perplexity and affliction), because some had misunderstood and mispractised and misapplied them. This, I say, made me much to suspect his sufficiency as for rightly understanding contemplative instructions in which and by which (as I had experienced for five or six years before) I could only prosper and live contented in my state. This, I say, I wondered at, because it did plainly appear that those who were weary of those instructions, in which others prospered so well, were for some notable reasons wholly incapable of benefitting themselves by such instructions, at least in these days when true spirituality hath so many oppositions and adversaries and so few that help and bear up a soul in them. And, I say, upon these terms such souls can never hold to them. And, therefore, it were fit (and he as fit as any) they should seek to be put into a more sensible course, which might be taught by man from time to time as they stood in need of. Whereas [for] others, who are truly capable of spiritual, contemplative instructions,

---

[81]   That is, 'unless'.

after the soul is once well instructed her director hath little to do but to rid her [of hindrances] in all things as much as he can lawfully and to refer her to God, who can only teach perfect prayer and bring the soul to true perfection. But those men who think themselves able to bring a soul to perfection of prayer by imposing their devices upon her and will limit God by their pretending that she is bound to obey them and can prosper by no other exercises than such as they seem to have found good by: from such men, I say, God bless all capable souls lest they put themselves into their hands. For if they under any pretence follow their inventions and leave the way that God hath placed them in and would prosper them by, the miserable effect will shew how little part God had in this their doing. For, as his works have most happy success, so ours have most woeful. And if we lay it upon obedience, we do God infinite wrong. Because the effect of obedience, if it be true obedience, is very profitable to a soul and never prejudicial. But it is when we *give that to Caesar that is God's* that it succeeds ill with us by obeying,[82] for by this pretended obedience we darken and obscure our soul contrary to God's meaning and intention. And it is always seen that, when a soul suffereth herself to be put out of her way by a director or superior, that when she thinks she hath done all she can as to the doing [of] their will, yet she is further from it than she was before, and both the superior and she miss of their desire. She, because she hath lost her peace, which made her capable of giving her superior his due without prejudice to her soul and of doing it as it was God's will she should, the which now she finds clean contrary by reason of her perverting the sweet order of justice, she being now so obscured that she knows not what to *give God* and what *Caesar*.[83] And by this means the superior also misseth of what he intended, because now the soul giveth him less than she did before.

---

82 See Matt 22:21; Mark 12:17; and Luke 20:25.
83 See Matt 22:21; Mark 12:17; and Luke 20:25.

We have infinite examples of the happy success of saints though their superiors were not always such as seconded them in all particulars, sometimes they being such as did not under-stand them and God permitting it for their greater good. And a soul shall always find contradiction from some superior or other. And yet, if the soul live in her interior as she should, it will be no impediment to her progress, no more than it was to Saint Teresa, John of the Cross, [or] Balthazar Alvarez of the Society of Jesus, who was persecuted by his order and his writings suppressed (as I have heard even to this day). And John of the Cross, besides other contradictions, [was] eight months put in prison by his superior. And these souls, though they might seem to others to have varied from true obedience, yet the effect shewed they were far from such matter. And these days there is in contemplative souls a more seeming disobedience than heretofore, because there are fewer superi-ors than ever there were that will concur or approve of their proceeding. But doth this exempt Religious from the right obedience more than heretofore? No, certainly. For there is no way but by obedience to come to God, and no virtue without obedience is pleasing to God. But it is an obedience that regardeth God and that doth what he would, and not a foolish pretended obedience which is in the *letter* and not in the *spirit*.[84] None can truly see how to obey but out of an internal light given and imparted to the soul by God, who is the true teacher of obedience and all other solid virtues. And in these days where true obedience is so little known and where obedience is counted to be practised in perfection when the subject is punctual out of a sympathy of nature with his superior and can by reason of a quiet nature magnify him and think that they must have no other relation to God in this world than by their superior, whom to please and whose good will and good word to enjoy is the perfection of what they came for without further acquaintance with God in their

[84]   See 2 Cor 3:6.

soul – this, I say, being now termed obedience, it is no wonder the world is so scarce of saints. God (I beseech him), teach us that obedience which is sound. For the other vanisheth away as smoke as to any solid effect in the soul.

It is an easy matter to talk and exhort souls to conform themselves in their interior to others where there is no obligation or any profit to come of it. And though it be against the stream of a true spirit and Call, and though he that thus adviseth us is here today and gone tomorrow, yet the perplexity that comes by such proceedings, if it be contrary to what God requires of us, may stick by us while we live to our great harm and grief. But were they that thus urge us (out of a certain custom) ever put to it themselves? No, surely. For if they had they would have more feeling of others being put out of their way. I speak not of a direct putting of a soul out, for that is too palpable of being ill, but of an indirect which pretendeth many things in excuse, and in particular more perfection, etc. But the poor soul, if she be by these pretenses put out of her way, will find herself both void of comfort, quiet, and perfection. For God never prospers indiscreet and inconsiderate proceedings, though we in them and for them be applauded by all the world. All that draws to multiplicity and estranging from God in our interior let us bless ourselves from as the poison of our soul, and any thing or creature that would interpose itself between God and our soul is an impediment to contemplation. Woe be to those souls, if they have a capacity for an internal life, that are studying how to write and speak to creatures to the pouring out of their affections. For by this means their affection will be taken up by the way, and the creatures will be more regarded than the Creator, though the subject of their writings be of and for God. Much vanity I have known in this kind, the ghostly father admiring the wit, devotion, and humility of his penitent. And the penitent, by having her proceedings in that kind admired, published, and applauded by her ghostly father, was in great danger to vanish away in her own cogitations. These sensible proceedings often draw the soul (do what she can) more to men than God.[85]

There are two things nowadays by which we take upon us to measure other men's perfection. The one is by the quiet-ness of their nature. And the other is, if we be superiors, we judge by the sympathy that is between them and us, terming them most humble, obedient, etc. that are most suitable to our spirit and sense. Those especially do so whose exercise is in sense and who put much perfection in sensible devotion. But certainly, true humility is so subtle a thing that none can judge who is most perfect therein but God and those to whom he revealeth it.[86] And this is the reason why it is said that the judgments of God are far different from those of men.[87]

Power was given by God for edification and not for destruction.[88] The which edification principally consisteth in the superior accommodating himself to the interior Divine Call of his subject. And with that intention are all Religious professions made and to be intended by the professors and acceptors of the profession, and especially according to the intention of our holy Mother the Church, by whose warrant those professions receive their validity. And therefore, a superior that neglects to proceed with his subjects according to such, their Divine Call accommodated to the Rule, strayeth from the scope and intention of Religious profession. And for the avoiding of these mischiefs, as also for the difficulty that superiors find and have in the true discovery of internal Calls that are of mere spiritual things, I may say was the cause wherefor the Holy Ghost (who is the proper master of true spirituality) hath inspired the pens of the torrent of his doctors of the holy Church to declare and teach that souls as well in Religion as out of it are free for their mere interior, whereby they may be

---

[85]   See Acts 5:29.
[86]   See Matt 11:27 and Luke 10:22.
[87]   See Isa 55:8.
[88]   2 Cor 10:8

able to follow such teaching from the Holy Ghost himself, as man cannot afford them. Though man may hurt or destroy such teachings easily where God permitteth it and [they] themselves yield to it to their own great loss and harm. And the interior is of that great and infinite worth and moment, that so that that may be well, it is no matter what cometh of all other things. Yea, then all other things will be well, if that be in good case by harkening to and following the divine interior Call, which is *all in all* to a capable soul.[89] O woe, woe, yea, a thousand times woe to a soul that is freighted by any threats, overcome by any temptations, or cast down by yielding to fears into that perplexity which maketh her unfit to hear and follow what God speaketh to her soul and disenableth her from following prayer, which Seraphinus Firmanus termeth, for the nobility and worth of it, 'omnipotent'![90] O you souls who are capable of prayer, be grateful to our Lord, for it is the greatest happiness that can be possessed in this life. For by it, it is easy passing through all things how hard and painful soever. By it we come to be familiar with God himself and to converse in heaven.[91] By it all impediments will be removed between God and our souls. By it we shall receive light for all that God would do by us. By it we shall come to regard God in all and wholly neglect ourselves. By it we shall know how to converse on earth without prejudice to our souls. And, in fine, by it we shall praise God and become so united to him that nothing shall be able to separate us for time or eternity from his sweet goodness. O let him *be all in all* to us,[92] who can only satisfy our souls. He is his own praise, in which and by which we are infinitely happy, though of ourselves we are able to praise and love him but in a very poor manner. Who can say (that desires nothing but to love and

---

[89]   1 Cor 15:28.
[90]   See note 51 above.
[91]   See Phil 3:20.
[92]   1 Cor 15:28.

praise him) that they are poor, seeing he who is more theirs than they are their own is so rich,[93] and to whom nothing is wanting that should make him an infinite happiness? In this let us joy,[94] in this let us glory without termination. When we are not able actually to attend to him and praise him, let us commend our heart and soul to the saints in heaven, who without ceasing praise our Lord. Let us by them do that which we are not able to do by ourselves. Yea, let us desire him (who is his own praise, who is only able to do as he deserveth) to supply what he desires we should wish him.

Let us rest in him alone and not in anything that is or can be created. Let us not seek the gift but the Giver. Let us seek no other comfort but to be able, without all comfort, to be true to him. O how little is all the love we can give him in comparison of that he deserveth from us. Where therefore is there room in our souls for any created thing? Let us wish and desire and, as far as it lies in us, procure that all love be given to him. Let him have all glory, all honour, and praise. Let us desire the favour of none but him alone, to whose free disposition let us stand for time and eternity as absolutely, by our will, as if we had never had being. Nothing we do or suffer let us esteem great, for our sins deserve we should endure much more. Let our whole care tend to the magnifying of him. Let his honour be ours, his glory ours, and let us seek nothing but to be wholly his who is most worthy to be that he is. It is his *delight to be with the children of men*.[95] What should comfort us but to praise and love him? Those that seek him shall find him if they seek him with all their heart. O, who would seek anything instead of him or anything besides him, [seeing] he is not more willing to give us anything than himself – here by grace and in heaven by glory? Let us *adore*

93 See ninth stanza of 'My God to Thee I Dedicate'.
94 'to feel or manifest joy; to be glad; to rejoice, exult'. See oed.com, s.v. 'joy', v. 2.a.
95 Prov 8:31.

him *in spirit and truth.*[96] All we can give him is nothing unless we entirely give him ourselves. And that also cannot add to his greatness and glory. Yet if we do this, so much doth his divine majesty esteem of this gift, it being all we can give him, that for it and in requital of it he will give us himself. All his gifts and graces are as means to preparing us for this end: if we use them rightly with humility and according to the just will of almighty God. Let us extend our will to serve, love, praise, please, and magnify our Lord to the uttermost we are able. Yea, without limits or bounds let us desire his honour till such time as we may be swallowed up in the bottomless ocean of all love, and praise God in himself – in whom and by whom only we can praise him as we ought. Let us love him here as far as we are possibly able, without regard of ourselves either for time or eternity. This is the humble love that feeleth no burden. This is the true love that knoweth not how to attribute anything it doth or suffereth to itself.[97] It chooseth not wherein God should make use of her but accommodateth itself to his pleasure in all things. If it were his will to have it so, she would rather forever be picking [up] chips or straws than out of her own election be doing that which is most admired or might seem to her to procure her the greatest reward. O you souls on whom God bestoweth this love: think it not much to bear the burden not only of yourselves but of all you live with. For God beareth you up in all, more than you can conceive or imagine! Beware above all things of pride, for that cast even angels out of heaven. A soul of prayer, as long as she keeps humility, is in little or no peril of going out of her way.

Give to Caesar that is Caesar's, and that to God that is God's.[98] If there be not something due to God which cannot be given

---

[96] John 4:24.
[97] See RB 4.42.
[98] See Matt 22:21; Mark 12:17; and Luke 20:25. The book indicates the passage from Matthew in a marginal note.

to men, or if it were so confused that there were no certainty what were due to the one – to wit, to God – and what were due for God to the other – to wit, man – a soul would be so confused as to teaching and leading the way of perfection that she would never know where to begin and where to end, or when she did well or ill. For certainly, when the soul doth that by men what ought to be done by God, and can be done by none but him, it goeth not well with her as for walking in a true contemplative course. She also doth not well when she would have God do that by himself which he would do by means of superiors or directors. And certainly, if a soul be a capable soul of contemplative instructions and be well grounded in them by help of one experienced, and walk the way of entire abnegation seeking God and not his gifts, and be diligent in observing what God will do by himself in her soul and wherein he refereth her to others, and walk with that indifference that it is all one to her which way or by whom God will manifest his will to her, she shall as easily see what and how to do in all things to please God best as she may discern the sun from the moon. And this is to *give that to God that is God's and that to Caesar's that is Caesar's.*[99]

The Interior or Spiritual Disposition[100]

 HE INTERIOR or SPIRITUAL DISPOSITION of man is of that great and infinite worth and moment that, so it be well, all other matters will also go well and

---

[99] See Matt 22:21; Mark 12:17; and Luke 20:25.
[100] The section in 1658 to which this short, informal treatise belongs is headed: 'Here follow some other sentences and sayings of the same pious soul found in some other papers of hers'.

97

be in good plight.[101] And the good state of the interior (and thereby also of the exterior) proceedeth from the harkening to and following of the divine interior Call (or inspiration). The which, to a soul capable of an internal life, is or ought to be as *all in all*.[102] And woe to such a soul who, overcome by threats or persuasions from without or by temptations within her or other occasions whatsoever, giveth over her prosecution of men^tal prayer, by means whereof only is she capable of discerning and following the divine will and Call. And therefore, O you souls that are capable of internal prayer, do you accordingly prosecute it and be grateful to God for the grace of it. For it causeth the greatest happiness that is to be gotten in this life and an answerable happiness in the future. For by it in this life one passeth through all things, how hard and painful soever they be. By it we become familiar even with God himself and [come] to have our *conversation in heaven*.[103] By it all impedi^ments will be removed between God and the soul. By it you shall receive light and grace for all that God would do by you. By it we shall come to regard God in all things and profitably neglect ourselves. By it we shall know how to converse on earth without prejudice to our souls. And, in fine, by it we shall praise God and become so united to him that nothing shall be able to separate us for time or eternity from his sweet goodness. And let him *be all in all* to us, who only can satisfy our souls.[104] He is his own praise, in which and by which we are infinitely happy, though of ourselves we are able to praise and love but in a very poor manner. Who can say (that desire nothing but to love and praise him) that they are poor, seeing he who is more theirs than they are their own is so rich[105] and to whom nothing is wanting that should make him an infinite happiness? In this

---

[101]   The first paragraph of the present treatise is intimately related to the third- and second-to-last paragraphs of the 'Apology'.

[102]   1 Cor 15:28.

[103]   Phil 3:20.

[104]   1 Cor 15:28.

[105]   See ninth stanza of 'My God to Thee I Dedicate'.

let us joy,[106] in this let us glory without intermission. When we are not able to attend unto him and praise him as we would, let us commend our heart and soul to the saints in heaven, who without ceasing praise our Lord. Let us do that by them which we are not able to do by ourselves. Yea, let us desire him who is his own praise and only is able to do it as he deserveth to have it done, to supply what he desireth we should wish him. Let us seek no other comfort but to be able without all comfort to be true to him. Let us rest in him alone and not in anything that is or can be created. Let us not seek the gift but the Giver. O, how little is all the love we can give him in comparison of that he deserveth from us? Where, therefore, shall there be room for any created thing in our souls? Let us wish and desire and (as far as it lies in us) procure that all love be given to him. Let him have all glory, all honour, and all praise. Let us desire the favour of none but him alone, to whose free disposition let us stand for time and eternity as absolutely by our will as if we never had any other freedom of will in us. Nothing we do or suffer let us esteem great, for our sins deserve much more. Let our whole care tend to the magnifying of him. Let his honour be ours, and let us seek nothing but to be wholly his who is most worthy to be that that he is. If it is his *delight to be with the children of men*, what should comfort us but to praise and love him?[107] Those that seek him shall find him with all their heart. O who would seek anything besides him, seeing he is not more willing to give us anything than his own self – here by grace and hereafter in heaven by glory? Let us *adore* him *in spirit and truth*.[108] All we can give him is nothing, unless we entirely give him ourselves, and that also cannot add to his greatness and glory. Yet, if we do this, so much doth his divine majesty esteem of this gift, that for it and in requital of it he will give us his own self. All his gifts and graces are a means

---

[106] 'to feel or manifest joy; to be glad; to rejoice, exult'. See oed.com, s.v. 'joy', v. 2.a.
[107] Prov 8:31.
[108] John 4:23 and 24.

for the preparing of us for this end, if we use them rightly with humility and according to the just will of Almighty God. Let us extend our will to serve, love, praise, please, and magnify our Lord to the uttermost we are able, yea, without all limits or bounds. Let us desire his honour till such time as we may be swallowed up in the bottomless ocean of all love, and praise God in himself – in whom and by whom and in whom only we can praise him as we ought. Let us love him as far as we are possible able, without regard for ourselves either for time or eternity. This is the humble love that feeleth no burden. This is the love that knoweth not how to attribute anything it doth or suffereth to itself.[109] It chooseth not wherein God shall make use of her but accommodateth herself in all things to his divine pleasure. If it were his will to have it so, she would rather forever be picking up chips or straws, than out of her own election to be doing that which is most admired or might seem to her to procure her the greatest reward. O you souls that God bestoweth his love upon: think it not much to bear the burden not only of yourselves but also of all that you live with. For God beareth you up in all, more than you can conceive or imagine. Beware above all things of pride, for that cast even angels out of heaven. A soul of prayer, as long as she keeps humility, is in no peril of going out of her way.

It is certainly true that God giveth himself to them who forsake all. I say all and not by halves, with reserving what we please to ourselves. But to all that forsake all, he giveth himself without exception of persons, and he that pleaseth our Lord needeth not fear all the devils in hell.

It is a wonderful thing to see the variety of opinions that are or may be about the best use of those things that of themselves are indifferent (or at least are not evil), one holding this and another that, every man according to his fancy and (as Saint Paul saith) *abounding in his own sense.*[110] No wonder

---

[109] See RB 4.42.
[110] Rom 14:5 (there is a marginal note in 1658 identifying this as Rom 4:3).

then that those that live and converse with others, and namely in a Religious community, do easily fall into occasion of jars[111] and differences with others, whilst everyone pretends the truth and the best to be of her side, howsoever it be indeed. And therefore, one's nature will easily take occasion of jarring with others, if it be not mortified by restraint from what it is inclining to by such occasions. It is only the divine virtue of true discretion that is able to discern and judge for one's own practice what is good, better, or best of all in the use of those different things. The more truly mortified the soul is, the clearer is such light of discretion in her and will increase in her, if she be still solicitous more and more to live to God in her interior and to die to herself and to all created things by simply regarding God in all she doth or emitteth, and intending him alone in all things.

It is a true proverb that it is an easier matter to corrupt the mind of one than of a great many. Wherefore, we must remember that *it is a good and happy thing for brethren to dwell* *in one* or rather (by true love and charity) in that *One which is* truly *necessary* – to wit, in God.[112] For no love is true but that which is in him and for him and without impediment to his love. All other loves are false, slippery, perverse, and vain, as not being founded in God, the ground of all true and happy love, nor being referred to him and his love. But the true love, which is the divine, will make all others dear unto us for his sake, and none dear but in him and for him. It will make us incapable of accounting any to be our enemies how hardly soever they treat us, because in all things we will regard God, that permitteth such difficulties to happen to us to the end our fidelity to him may thereby be tried. And so [we should] not regard (with any aversion) the party who afflicteth us. And it will be sufficient for us towards the pacification of our soul, upon the hard or bitter usage offered us, that we remember

[111] 'discord, divergence'. See oed.com, s.v. 'jar', II.
[112] Ps 133:1 and Luke 10:42.

that he hath suffered it to happen to us for our good, who only knoweth what is best for the humbling of us and the abating of our pride. The which must be done if [we] will be pleasing to God, to whom now and ever I commit myself. Amen.

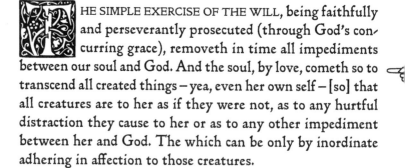

A Poesy

num sit mihi totum, id est, omnia in omnibus. Let one be all to me, that is, *all in all.*[113] This was a poesy bestowed on me and my partners by another, the truth whereof I pray God may answerably be in the hearts and loves of us, and of all other souls whatsoever.

The Simple Exercise of the Will

THE SIMPLE EXERCISE OF THE WILL, being faithfully and perseverantly prosecuted (through God's concurring grace), removeth in time all impediments between our soul and God. And the soul, by love, cometh so to transcend all created things – yea, even her own self – [so] that all creatures are to her as if they were not, as to any hurtful distraction they cause to her or as to any other impediment between her and God. The which can be only by inordinate adhering in affection to those creatures.

---

[113]   1 Cor 15:28.

A True Spiritual, Internal Life

 TRUE SPIRITUAL, INTERNAL LIFE is so private and secret between God and the soul that others cannot easily discern it – no, not by the external effects of it. For in her exterior carriage she is common and general, as hating singularity, by means whereof she avoideth much occasion of pride and walketh the more securely between God and her.

Those that Live an Internal Life

 HOSE THAT LIVE AN INTERNAL LIFE do so withdraw all natural, inordinate affection from creatures that they often therefore are censured by superiors and equals to[114] neglect others out of pride. But they, abhorring to have special interest in any, do proceed so far as they can according to true charity and mind not what others judge of them, they desiring only in all to discharge their duty to God, whom they regard in all things. And as they have interest in none, so not any hath interest in them. In that which they propose to superiors, they proceed (as in all things else) with all sincerity, detesting the contrary practice, even with those that are most adverse and contrary to them – much more with superiors. And whatsoever they desire to do, they do it with such an indifferency that what event soever come of it, they remain in peace, embracing it as God's will, whose will is their law. If that which they propose, either for the common good and peace of the house or for their own good, do not seem fit in true justice or reason to superiors to be

---

[114] That is, 'as if they'.

granted, they importune no farther nor desire the favour of being condescended to in their motion, but rather (remaining themselves indifferent) that they determine and proceed in it, to whom[115] it appertaineth.

A superior hath great reason to take heed of putting a soul from the exercise of her internal prayer or so overcharging her with labours or solicitudes that she cannot become recollected in her daily prayer, it being a soul that hath aptness in her to make spiritual progress by prayer and the other exercises of a contemplative life. Yea, not only the soul herself will feel the unspeakable damage that will come to her thereby, but also the superior himself, in the obedience which he expecteth and is due to him from her, will see the harm and loss that cometh by such bereaving of the soul of her prayer. For she, who would by discreet prosecuting a course of mental prayer, have become subject (if it were necessary) even to the creature that is of the least esteem or worth in the world, becometh now for want of that strength and help which is gotten by such prayer to be almost impossible to be ruled by the wisest man in the world. For living in Religion (as I can speak by experience), if one be not in a right course of prayer and other exercises between God and our soul, one's nature groweth much worse than ever it would have been if she had lived in the world. For pride and self-love, which are rooted in our soul by sin, findeth means to strengthen itself exceedingly in one in Religion, if she be not in a course that may teach her and procure her true humility. For by the corrections and contradictions of the will (which cannot by any be avoided but will be, living in a Religious community), I found my heart grown, as I may say, as hard as a stone, and nothing would have been able to have mollified it but by being put into a course of prayer by which a soul tendeth towards God and learneth of him the lesson of truly humbling herself. In which course being placed and ever tending to the increase of

---

[115] That is, 'the superiors'.

humility, even the defects and errors she committeth either out of frailty or ignorance do turn to her gain, as giving her occasion of the greater humbling of herself to and under God. And humility and the love of God (wherein all her good con-sisteth) do each of them increase the one the other, for they are inseparable companions.[116]

It is the grace of God and tending to him by way of love that only can so enable a soul that no difficulty or disgrace can happen which she is not prepared for, and therefore [she] is able willingly to embrace the same. Verily, I can affirm this by mine own experience, that a cross word or slight reprehension, before I got into this spiritual course, was more insupportable to me and did more disquiet my mind than all the difficulties or disgraces which since have fallen upon me have done. For now, methinks, though I be neglected by all the world, yet by flying to our Lord he easeth me of all my burthen. And as I have desired to have no other friend or comforter but him, so it pleaseth him neither in doubts, fears, pains, disgraces, nor in any other miseries (whereunto this life of ours is so subject) to reject me. Only he exacts of me that in all the contradictions of will he sends me or permits to fall on me, I will humble myself and be confident in his help. Of which, if I do so, I shall be much more sure than if in mine own hands I had a most absolute power.[117]

None are able to prosecute the way of the divine love but they who are resolved to deny themselves in all things and who willingly and wittingly adhere to no created thing. For if the soul do willingly retain an affection to any such thing, she is at a stop and can go no further. For God must be sought and loved wholly, if we desire to arrive to perfection.[118]

<hr />

[116] Parts of this paragraph are related to the 'Apology', paragraphs 6 and 7.
[117] Parts of this paragraph are related to the 'Apology', paragraphs 10 and 11
[118] Parts of this paragraph are related to the 'Apology', paragraph 47(taking the numbered sections after the internal subtitle as one paragraph).

The Sanctity of the Old Orders[119]

HEN ONLY THE HONOUR OF GOD was sin‑ cerely – without intermingling of human ends or interests – intended and sought, and all orders with one consent of heart did concur to the advancement of that alone. They then applied themselves to several exercises in the exterior, everyone according to his institute – some more easy and some more strict, some of more action and some of less. Yet interiorly their principle end was all one, and that was to find and enjoy God in their souls. And out of that perfect charity, which especially by those their internal exercises did grow in them, they did everyone, as God did require and enable them, employ part of their time in gaining or doing good to other souls. Then there was no great care or solicitude about temporalities, God taking care and being, as it were, solicitous of them. Then there was indeed all sincere and real proceedings between them. Then there was per‑ fect amity without proper interest or fond affection to the impediment of their loving and seeking after God alone, who is that *One thing* which only *is necessary.*[120] Then there was no acceptation of persons, but they were contented so [long as] God's honour were advanced, not caring though it were done by any other order as well as by themselves. O Lord my God, if this spirit might be revived again, how much would my soul rejoice! If Saint Benedict his, Saint Francis his, Saint Ignatius his, etc., children were perfectly (as this life will permit) united together and [did] with one heart and consent, seek, and labour to advance thy honour and praise as our founders do in heaven, [...] then would the spirit of the primitive Church flourish and thy torn and mangled mem‑

---

[119]   1658 includes the following heading for this text: 'She, speaking of the sanctity of the old orders in old time, when they were in their best case or in the prime of their good spirits, writeth and sayeth as followeth, viz.'

[120]   See Luke 10:42.

bers be healed and perfectly set again together. Then heretics and sinners would easily be converted by them to thee. Then there would be another learning than now doth flourish in our order. And thou by them wouldst speak, *who makest the tongues of infants eloquent*.[121] Then they by prayer, convers-ing in a familiar and tender manner with thee, would speak so that none would be able to resist thee in them.[122] Then their judgement would be so cleared that they would under-stand most hidden mysteries. Then an hour of prayer would instruct them more full than fifty years study can do, they having by the means of such prayer (in all things) relation to thee, the only true wisdom and *in whose light* only is true *light* to be seen.[123] By loving thee and dying to themselves in all things, they would become masters of themselves. And all the world would then nothing move them nor would any-thing affright them, because thou wouldst be their stay and comfort in all things.[124]

If we will do as we ought and as is best for us, we must be subject to the will of God in all things without exception. And this is the benefit of an internal life: that it makes one capable of seeing and knowing God's will and also most ready to perform it, which way soever he signify it to them, which makes them obey as readily and willingly (merely for God's sake and out of obedience to him) a simple or imper-fect superior as they would an angel or the wisest creature in the world. Yea, if it were possible that a worm or any other creature were ordained by God to rule over them, they would with all their hearts embrace his will by them, for without this total subjection to God, it is impossible to become truly spiritual. For if we resist his will in our superiors, in vain do we pretend to please him. This virtue therefore of obe-

---

121 Wis 10:21.
122 See Luke 21:15.
123 See Ps 36:9.
124 Parts of this paragraph are related to the 'Apology', paragraph 61(taking the numbered sections after the internal subtitle as one paragraph).

dience we must learn of him. The which must be grounded upon true humility, that must be our stay in all things. And those two virtues of humility and obedience, together with the divine virtue of discretion, he will teach us, if we do our parts in seeking to become more and more humble and subject to him. For seeing it is his will we should obey and become truly humble, how can we doubt but he will give us the grace, if we humbly and perseverantly beg it of him and practise those virtues upon occasions as well as we can? For he himself hath said, *When we ask our father bread, he doth not give a stone, nor if we ask him fish, will he give a serpent.*[125] Much less will he deny us what is necessary to make us pleasing to him, and[126] we [seek] or [desire] nothing but by true love to be faithful to him. O prayer, prayer, able to obtain all things! O how cometh it to pass, my Lord, that this omnipotent thing (as some of thy dear servants term it), prayer, should be so unknown — yea, and even to them whom thou termest *the salt of the earth*,[127] contemned (I mean mental prayer) at least for the practice of poor simple women, for whom they hold it above all things most dangerous, even to my own knowledge, as I have known affirmed by superiors of several orders! O misery to be truly lamented by all that have or may have taste in prayer and [that] by the effect thereof know how sweet a thing it is to attend only and wholly to the praise and love of God! Surely, the want of the wisdom which by prayer the saints did gain is the cause why custom and opinion do take place (for the most part in this world) of true reason. Surely, never was the world reformed of its sins and errors, but it must be by the wisdom which cometh from God and is far different from that which is

---

125 Luke 11:12.
126 'if; suppose that, provided that, on condition that'. See oed.com, s.v. 'and' II.a.
127 See Matt 5:13.

accounted *wisdom* by the *world*, which, as Saint Paul saith, is *folly before God.*[128]

---

[128] 1 Cor 3:19. Parts of the present paragraph are intimately related to the sixty-second and sixty-third paragraphs of the 'Apology' (taking the numbered sections after the internal subtitle as one paragraph).

FURTHER READING

EDITIONS OF DAME GERTRUDE MORE'S WORKS

Baker, Augustine. *Confessiones Amantis: The Spiritual Exercises of the Most Vertuous and Religious Dame Gertrude More*, ed. John Clark. Salzburg: Institut für Anglistik und Amerikanistik, Salzburg University, 2007.

More, Gertrude. *The Early Modern Englishwoman*, series II, part 4, vol. 3, ed. Arthur F. Marotti [reissue of *The spiritual exercises of the most virtvovs and religious D. Gertrvde More*]. Farnham: Ashgate, 2009.

—— *The spiritual exercises of the most vertvovs and religious D. Gertrvde More of the holy order of S. Bennet and English congregation of Our Ladies of Comfort in Cambray*. Paris, 1658.

—— *The Writings of Dame Gertrude More*, rev. and ed. Dom Benedict Weld-Blundell. London: R. & T. Washbourne, 1910.

STUDIES AND CONTEXT

Baker, Augustine. *Idiot's Devotion: Directions*, ed. James Clark. Salzburg: Institut für Anglistik und Amerikanistik, Salzburg University, 2008.

—— *The Life and Death of Dame Gertrude More*, ed. Ben Wekking. Salzburg: Institut für Anglistik und Amerikanistik, Salzburg University, 2002.

The Benedictines of Stanbrook. *In a Great Tradition: Tribute to Dame Laurentia McLachlan, Abbess of Stanbrook*. London: John Murray, 1956.

Goodrich, Jaime. '"Low and Plain Stile": Poetry and Piety in English Benedictine Convents, 1600–1800'. *British Catholic History*, vol. 34, no. 4, 2019, pp. 599–618.

Hall, Jeremy. 'Dame Gertrude More: The Living Tradition'. In *Medieval Women Monastics: Wisdom's Wellsprings*, ed. Miriam Schmitt and Linda Kulzer. Collegeville, MN: Liturgical Press, 1996.

Heale, Martin. *Monasticism in Late Medieval England, c. 1300–1535*. Manchester: Manchester University Press, 2009.

Kelly, James E., and Susan Royal, eds. *Early Modern English Catholicism: Identity, Memory, and Counter-Reformation*. Leiden: Brill, 2017.

Knowles, David. *The Religious Orders in England: Volume III the Tudor Age*. Cambridge: Cambridge University Press, 1959.

Latz, Dorothy. '*Glow-Worm Light* ...': *Writings of Seventeenth-Century English Recusant Women from Original Manuscripts.* Salzburg: Institut für Anglistik und Amerikanistik, Salzburg University, 1989.

—— 'The Mystical Poetry of Dame Gertrude More'. *Mystics Quarterly*, vol. 16, no. 2, June, 1990, pp. 66–82.

Lawrence, C. H. *Medieval Monasticism.* 3rd edn. Harlow: Longman, 2001.

Lux-Sterritt, Laurence. *English Benedictine Nuns in Exile in the Seventeenth Century: Living Spirituality.* Manchester: Manchester University Press, 2017.

Sandeman, Frideswide. *Dame Gertrude More.* Leominster: Gracewing, 1997.

Stanbrook Abbey: A Sketch of its History 1625–1925. London: Burns, Oates & Washbourne, 1925.

Walker, Claire. *Gender and Politics in Early Modern Europe: English Convents in France and the Low Countries.* London: Palgrave MacMillan, 2003.

Milton Keynes UK
Ingram Content Group UK Ltd.
UKHW010717180823
427095UK00001B/55

9 780852 449431